FREE BONUS:
YOUR SHADOW WORK STARTER KIT

Uncover What's Really Holding You Back — and Heal It

This book is more than words on a page. It's a gateway to the inner transformation you've been avoiding. To help you begin that journey with support and power, I've created a free companion bundle to go beyond the pages.

Download your FREE Shadow Work Starter Kit at:
www.JasonBKendrick.com/ShadowBonus

Inside your Shadow Work Starter Kit, you'll get:

- *The Inner Child Reconnection Guide* — start healing the hidden pain you've buried for too long
- Exclusive Excerpt from *"It's Not Your Life, It's You"* — the next step in your healing journey
- A Private Invitation to Book a Shadow Strategy Session with Jason — limited availability

Start your healing journey now — visit
www.JasonBKendrick.com/ShadowBonus

FACING
THE
DEVIL
IN
YOU

FACING
THE
DEVIL
IN
YOU

JASON B. KENDRICK

Breckenridge, Colorado

Book design by Journey Bound Publishing

Published by Blue Boy Media LLC

ISBN: 979-8-9995273-0-1
Library of Congress Control Number: 2025914998

*To my Mother, Nancy, without whom
I would Literally not be here. But more
importantly, for your sharing of your
passions and for taking me with you to so
many magical places and introducing me
to the people who became my Mentors,
Teachers, Friends and Family.*

*Without you and your loving influence,
this book would never have come to be and
my life would be vastly different… And,
probably not in a good way. You have been
my Rock, Shoulder, Travel Companion,
Bank and so much more.*

*This book is for you. I love you
and thank you.*

Jason

"Facing the devil in you" can be understood as confronting inner struggles, negative thoughts, or temptations, often framed within a religious or spiritual context, where the "devil" represents forces of evil, your shadow side or your personal negativity in thoughts and beliefs."

—

"The Devil/Demons are simply a manifested projection from the negative side of the collective consciousness of humanity. They are not independent entities, in their own right."

— Quote from a Bashar channeling.

CONTENTS

INTRODUCTION

I f you are struggling in life, it is probably because you haven't figured out your innate gifts, wholeness, and uniqueness, and you still think life is supposed to be a struggle.

First off, you are a divine creation of the creator, God if you prefer; that is unique, one of a kind and irreplaceable, with a set of gifts and traits that are as unique as you are. No two people are alike on this planet, much less in the universe. You are all living in a specially designed personal universe of your very own. And you are the creator of it, so, if you don't like it you can complain to management, just find your nearest mirror.

Yes, many of us have similarities and if we so choose, we can stuff ourselves into any number of differing categories, boxes, criteria, or whatever you choose to define yourself. Those similarities are the things that give us common ground upon which to relate to one another.

Birds of a feather flock together because we are social creatures and need social interaction. As well, we are energetic vibrational beings who instinctively know that by coming together in groups, we harmonize and amplify our energies. Max Planck, the father of Quantum

Physics, called this the "Master Mind." The Bible even states that: "when two or more are gathered in my name, I will be there..." (Matthew 18:20, KJV). This alludes to the power of the group mind or consciousness.

We are universally unique beings craving social interaction with others, a dichotomy in terms, if I've ever heard one.

Why is it that we as unique beings seek interaction and validation from others who may be similar but never exactly like us?

Why is it that when we put others' opinions ahead of our own, that we suffer?

Why is it that we believe only certain parts of ourselves are valuable and beneficial and other parts are bad and detrimental?

How can we believe so many strange things when we all know, at a deeply spiritual and personal level, that the creator makes no mistakes, including us?

These are the questions I hope to answer, address and, if at all possible, dispel altogether within these pages. We are going to have a conversational journey together into the depth of our uniqueness and into the universal truths that we have yet to learn, having been lied to about and/ or misdirected away from them by well-meaning parents and elders, power-hungry greedy capitalists and those of differing belief systems who cannot abide without their particular brand of beliefs.

For those of you who are experiencing me for the first time, welcome! I am not your conventional writer, speaker, healer, person, man, human… I have tried for most of my life to be what I thought I was supposed to be, and in every instance, I met with failure. Recently, the universe has had a grand time of showing me, reminding me and downright browbeating me into the understanding that I can be no one other than the unique little snowflake that I am. So, here I am once again spewing my words onto these pages for you and yours to read. I do not follow standard English literary paradigms, as anyone with a middle school education has probably already figured out. I write the way I think, the way I speak and in a manner which is uniquely my own, basically because I can't do it any other way.

That being said, what is written here will resonate with many of you. Many of you will resist much of what is written here. Many of you won't be able to get anything out of the concepts within this book because of my lousy grammar, punctuation, and vocabulary. I accept all of that and ask that if this book has landed in your lap, please do your best to get through it with an open mind and heart. Though I am no English major or scholar, I do bring a lot to the table that, if given the opportunity to flower within you, can create major life-affirming changes in you. I only ask that you give these words a chance and then pass them along to the next person who comes along and shows interest.

I am all about raising the vibrations of our community, world, planet, and universe. This is done by coming together as unique individuals with like thoughts and intentions. Sometimes that can be done with the sharing of a book, like this one, thoughts or just a hug. We are in this together and though I may not be your standard cup of tea, I hope you'll gain something from these pages and will share them with someone. In so doing, we all do our little part to raise our world up into the wholeness and magic that the creator made possible for us to enjoy.

Now, let's get this rollercoaster started up the tracks... Hang on to your preconceived notions and ingrained thought patterns... This is going to be a bumpy ride!!

WHO I AM AND WHY I'M WRITING THIS

F or those of you that like to relate to the authors you read or who are wondering what makes me qualified to write this book, this is for you.

Alternatively, if you are one who doesn't care about the author's story and just want to get to the meat of the book, feel free to skip to Chapter One.

MY STORY:

I'm not really sure how to begin or how to make this a succinct accounting of my life in such a way that will relate to the book's subject matter in a way that will prove to you in any way that my experiences in this life have made me an expert in Facing my own Devil and authorize me to write this book.

All I can do is give you an account of who I am and how I got here. I will do my best to keep it from too many rabbit holes and ramblings as I proceed, but I will warn you, this tale will not be free of rabbit holes or ramblings.

It is always hardest to begin, so I will start at what I consider my beginning in relation to this story.

I hope you are familiar with my other works, so that this introduction doesn't overly tax your beliefs and hold on reality.

To begin I will go back, WAY BACK, to a Galaxy Far, Far Away and to my lives lived in the Orion Constellation as a Padawan, Jedi, Sith, Wiseman, Elder, Imperial Officer and regular person just trying to live my life.

Yes, I am referring to George Lucas's Star Wars movies. The reason is that those movies are a download from the Orion Constellation from a long time ago when that system was living under a tyrannical rule of what George calls "The Empire."

These movies are the Orion Federation's attempt to educate Earth Humanity on the dangers of Dualism and Dualistic thinking. The Light and The Dark sides are two sides of the Whole that is God, or the ALL, if you prefer that.

As the source expanded and created more and more experiences of creation, dualistic thinking and dualism became a great challenge to the expansion of the All. This separation from the mind of wholeness to one of light and dark, right and wrong, strength over peace, control over freedom causes millennia of turmoil and strife across an entire universe and dimension.

I bring this concept up, because I was there, in many different and varied incarnations during those times. I played every role I could to learn as much as I could about Dualism and its effects on spiritual expansion and growth.

As an Emissary from Orion, coming to Earth to attempt to help stop what happened in the Orion System from happening here as well. I have spent lifetime after lifetime as a spiritual teacher and agent of expansion and change. It has not gone well…

I've been the Christlike figure, Pharoah, Shaman, Warrior Priest, Cobbler, Baker and Candlestick maker… I have lived so many lives on Earth attempting to open eyes and hearts to the dangers of Dualism and Separation that I often forget I've been anywhere else.

I'm sure it won't take too much of your imagination to guess how many of those incarnations went. I've been criticized, belittled, disrespected, demeaned, laughed at, ostracized, imprisoned, tortured, beheaded, crucified and so on for attempting to help and inspire humanity to wholeness and connection with each other and the one true Source.

And, so, here I am again, once again attempting to inspire and encourage wholeness, one mind at a time.

I've been told that this time it is safe to share and that this time we will prevail over dualism, darkness, and fear. Though, to be perfectly honest, I am still terrified to share these same topics that cause me so much pain and grief in past incarnations.

Yet, this is my job and what I keep signing up for, because I believe in my soul that it is worth it to awaken humanity to the Magic of Wholeness and Connection with oneself, our Human Family and our Source. We are all One; of and by The One True Source of Creation.

We are the droplet of water that makes up the Ocean of the One.

Rabbit hole #1 complete!

So, as an Emissary from Orion, here to teach Oneness and Wholeness once again, I have hope that this life will turn out better than the others.

In this incarnation I chose to be born into a Southern military family from Texas.

My parents had me when they were both twenty-three years old and my father was in the Army. We traveled to Wurzburg, Germany when I was around six months old. My mother soon joined the Army as well and began her career as a Psych-Nurse in the Service.

We moved back to Texas when I was four and my father left the Army. We lived near San Antonio for about a year before moving out into the country of Bexar County, where I began school at age five.

With my parents' upbringings, me being the only child, my nature as an Old Soul, the societal norms of the late '70s and '80s, i.e.: latchkey kids, both parents working, the ideology of "kids are meant to be seen and not heard," shame as a method of parenting, etc.. I spent a lot of my early years on my own and learning to take care of myself.

When my parents separated, I was around six years old, and this event caused a lot of trauma for me, much of which I didn't become aware of until many decades later. Not to mention the effects of my past life experiences and what those unconscious memories created within me. Due to all that and more, I developed a highly independent nature, which still holds sway for me today.

I am a natural introvert and a deep thinker. I'm empathic and very intuitive. One term that helps to describe me is that of an Indigo Child. If you Google Indigo Children, this is what you'll get back.

In a New Age spiritual context, "indigo child" refers to a child believed to possess unique, often supernatural, traits or abilities, sometimes associated with an indigo-colored aura. The term emerged from a pseudoscientific concept and is often used to describe children who exhibit unusual psychological traits or behaviors.

Key Characteristics and Beliefs:

Unique Abilities:

Indigo children are believed to have heightened sensitivity, intuition, creativity, and a strong sense of purpose.

Psychological Traits:

They are often described as challenging societal norms, questioning authority, and having a strong need for independence and self-expression.

Aura:

Some believe indigo children possess a prominent indigo-colored aura, a spiritual energy field.

"System Busters":

They are sometimes seen as "system busters" who challenge the status quo and strive to create a more harmonious and equitable world.

Higher Consciousness:

The concept often suggests that indigo children are "highly evolved" individuals with a deeper understanding of the world.

If you are familiar with Delores Canon and her work with the Convoluted Universe Book Series or her Quantum Healing Hypnosis Technique therapy and past life regressions and investigations, you may have heard of her book, *The Three Waves of Volunteers*.

In that book, she describes Three Waves of Volunteers that have come to incarnate on the planet in the last hundred years to help with humanity's awakening and ascension into 5th density consciousness and the New Earth Paradigm.

I fall into the Second Wave Volunteer category and if you Google that, this is what you'll get back.

In Dolores Cannon's theory, the "Second Wave" of volunteers refers to individuals who are considered to have made a more seamless transition to life on Earth than the first wave. They are described as often working behind the scenes, channeling energy onto Earth like antennas, and their energy is said to unconsciously affect those around them, according to the Second Wave: Transcending the Human Drama book.

Hidden Role:

Second wave volunteers often operate in the background, working independently and creating little to no karma.

Energy Channeling:

They are described as unconscious energy conduits, much like antennas, passively channeling energy into the Earth's system.

Influence and Paradox:

Their energy is said to impact those they interact with, but they are often described as not liking being around people, creating a paradox of sharing energy while being solitary.

Service and Purpose:

They are seen as old souls and master teachers from other galaxies, called to Earth for the transition into the Age of Aquarius. Their purpose is to help humanity awaken and transcend the human drama.

If you are keeping score so far, that means that I am an Emissary/Starseed from Orion, an Indigo Child/Adult, and a Second Wave Volunteer here to assist with humanity's ascension and transformation out of separation into wholeness.

I am passionate about the future and health of humanity in such a way that I have found it hard to form long term relationships due to my otherworldly focus on ascension. It is hard to accept the "Normal" nine-to-five grind and white picket fence family when I cannot abide by or accept the societal norms and collective consciousness of separation and dualism on this planet at this time.

Believe me, I have tried and failed miserably to be a normal person following the prescribed notion of normalcy. It just doesn't fit nor resonate with my soul nor my purpose here on Planet Earth.

I have wished many, many times throughout my life that I could just "fit in" and follow the tide. I just can't. My soul won't allow it, and to be honest, I wouldn't make a very good Muggle anyway.

To add to my oddities as a Human, I will also add in my Human Design characteristics for you to better understand the path of my life so far and why I am now, at fifty, coming out full force to fulfill my purpose this lifetime.

Generator 4/6s are designed to connect and influence the people they cultivate a friendliness or familiarity with.

Up until age 30, you're trying a lot of different things so that you can eventually achieve perfection. You sample lots of different relationships and experiences so that you have lots to digest as you mature.

From 30 to 50, you are designed to take a step back, hang at the edge of the group as a voyeur (literally and figuratively), and reflect on everything you've learned.

At age 50, you step into your full capacity as a Role Model—someone who has been there, done that, and taken plenty of time to figure out not only what works but what is perfect. At this point, you understand who you are, and you're showing up in the world with integrity, as that person.

You are here to influence others and allow your connections to bring you opportunities and assistance in meeting your goals. Through your relationships, you make your dreams happen, learn about yourself, live your purpose, and inspire others to do the same, just by being you.

Honestly, I'm not so sure how I feel about this whole "Role Model" thing. I would never consider myself any type of role model to anyone else. I just have to trust in the wisdom of the divine that this is for the best.

What I can say, which falls right in line with this book and its concept of Facing the Devil in You, is that once you do your inner work and integrate your shadow side and inner child exiles, you feel much more solid and more like a foundational leader who can help others through your past experiences.

With my own shadow side and inner child exiles in a constant state of integration, I can better and more confidently stand in my truth of who I am and share that with this world full of naysayers, critics, trolls and fear mongering control freaks.

All the things I used to hide from the world in shame and fear of judgment and ridicule, I now use to connect with others in our work of integration and re-parenting our inner children. The magic of wholeness is the power that you gain when you are fully integrated and no longer trying to hide parts of you from the world around you.

This has been my experience, and what has transformed me from the weak little nice guy, people-pleasing my way through the world, into someone who can stand strong in my convictions and weather any judgments that come my way. This is what I want for you who are reading this book to gain for yourselves.

My Devil and Shadow side have become my superpower to share with the world. The more I have learned to accept and integrate all those parts of me that I used to judge and hide from myself and all those around me, the more authentic, effective, and successful I have become in my life.

To be fully transparent and truthful to you, my reader, who is trusting me with your time and attention, I will give you a little synopsis of my personal Devil and how he serves me today.

MY PARENTS AND UPBRINGING:

My parents were born in the '50s, grew up in the '60s and were young adults in the swinging '70s. Their lives were full of free love and sexual experimentation. I cannot say for sure but, I believe now that, my father was in full-fledged sex addiction by the time I came along. He had many girlfriends and lots of experiences within and outside of his marriage.

One of his parental mistakes, as I see it today, was the fact that he left his porn tapes out where they were easily accessible to me as a kid and at about five years old, my sexual education began.

I'm not sure I truly understood all I saw on those tapes, but they sure lit a fire in me to experience what I saw. I began to experiment with my little friends who came over for sleepovers, attempting to mimic what I saw on those tapes.

It also taught me that sex and sexuality were secretive dirty things that you kept hidden in the closet or cabinet out of sight and didn't talk about. My parents didn't talk to me about sex or porn or any aspect of those topics except to laugh and make little jokes about my "Favorite Tapes and Magazines," as my dad was packing up his stuff when he moved out of the house.

Wait, that's not completely accurate; my mom did ask me once when I was about nine if I knew where babies came from. After I laughed, I said, "Yes, I know...". No, I didn't have the proper sexual education, but I was sure educated.

This early exposure and improper sexual education led me down my own road of sex and porn addiction. Of course, there was no such thing as sex addiction or porn addiction in the '80s and '90s. I was just a hedonistic, voyeuristic explorer with no one to guide me or teach me. I was on my own and drowning in an ever-growing sea of addiction. And once the internet hit home in the mid '90s, oh brother, all bets were off.

I had no true connections in my relationships and was only interested in my next conquest. In my earliest sexual fantasies, I knew nothing about love or intimacy. It was just about getting to experience what I saw in porn and what I imagined that to be like.

I was obsessed and fascinated by all things sex, like most teenaged boys are, but I had no foundation of anything resembling healthy sexuality and/or intimacy and what that meant. For me, it was just the physical act and how many girls I could get to experience it with.

I moved with my dad, his new wife, and new stepsister to Germany when I was twelve turning thirteen. My dad had rejoined the Army after a layoff and we were stationed in Germany again.

I should mention that my stepmother was not thrilled with the fact that I was there. She had it in mind when she and my dad married that it would just be her, my dad, and her daughter from her previous marriage. She was not expecting, nor wanting, his son to join her happily little family unit.

Once we were all in Germany, the fun did begin. I received less than favorable treatment from my stepmother while she fawned over and spoiled my stepsister. I'm sure they would disagree, but that was my experience at that time.

Also, in a move of sheer forethought and brilliance, my father moved us to a little German town 40 kilometers away from base and all the other American kids. So, as a twelve, soon to be thirteen-year-old boy, pulled away from all my friends I'd had and moved to a foreign county. I didn't speak the language and had no friends outside of school, which was a 45-minute bus ride to and from.

As you can imagine, I got into a bit of trouble that year. I lusted over a young GI's German wife who lived across from us and got into his and another American neighbor's porn stashes before being caught by his wife in the other neighbor's home watching his porn.

Oh, and lest I forget, as a hormonal and pubescent boy of twelve or thirteen, with ready access to porn from my father and neighbors, with no outlet or access to young ladies my age to express myself or experiment with, I looked for other outlets near at hand. I spied on my stepmom in the shower, as well as other lewd teenage acts that I'll not repeat here. Of course, I got caught and was sent to a counselor to try to heal my deviant behavior.

Luckily for me, the counselor saw me as I was, a young boy in the throes of puberty with healthy curiosities and no real outlet for them. The porn wasn't really addressed and, looking back, I wish it had been, but everything has its own time and place to be addressed.

My father didn't take any of this very well and did as most parents would when afraid of what it all might mean: he made it worse. Through shame, punishment and forced counseling sessions, I retreated even further inward and vowed to never let them find out about anything else I did. The shame and self-hatred I developed during that time was eventually masked by my first forays into drinking, partying, and sex.

During my counseling, the therapist did take an interest in my stepmother and either he or another subsequent therapist diagnosed her with bipolar and manic-depressive disorder. Add that to my dad's either hands-off or overly critical approach to parenting, and I began to isolate and hide more and more. Much of it, I believe, was normal teenage angst and independence-seeking, but in hindsight, I can see how extreme some of my hiding behaviors became during that time.

But, as an old country song might say, it got worse before it got better.

My first sexual experience was during a house party with an ex-girlfriend of one of the older boys I skateboarded with and idolized. It didn't go to plan.

We were young, horny and drunk and it seemed like a good idea at the time, but halfway through losing my virginity, she began to cry and ask me if I was done yet. She was crying and calling herself a whore for doing this with me and well, as you can imagine, I didn't really take that well.

All my fantasies of this magical moment of sex were dashed and, in their place, I put shame, fear and self-judgment. These feelings didn't diminish my sexual fantasies or desires. No, in many ways, they intensified them. I was now committed to "Do It Right" next time.

Can you guess how "Next Time" went?

Yep, not well. My second sexual experience was with a senior cheerleader girl. That's right, not just an older woman, but a cheerleader and a senior!! WHAT?! I know right, stud material in the making!

However, in my over-exuberance, lack of experience, and this being only my second time, I lasted about twenty or thirty seconds. She laughed at me and said, "Well, at least you found the hole…"

OMG! Crushed! I failed again, and she laughed at me to add insult to injury.

This did nothing to assuage my budding sexual addiction. In contrast, it reinforced my desire, now blooming into a need, to be good at sex and make the girls crazy in bed. I wanted to be a Sex God like I saw in those porn tapes. Which, as we all know, is totally real and not acting at all…

I vowed to become good in bed, nah, Great in Bed, and to make all the girls scream. Can you guess how that went?

Looking back now, I cringe, but I cannot help but see the correlation between my dad's addiction and my own. I mean, in a strange way, that was all we had in common in the first place. It was an unspoken connection between father and son. Something we had in common and even if unspoken, it was a connection to my father that I was desperately looking for.

It was also my vain attempt to fill the intimacy hole that was growing in my heart. Sex or the searching for it was the only way I knew to assuage the emptiness I was feeling.

I should add in here that my parents' upbringings in 1950s central Texas were not the stuff of sitcoms like Leave It to Beaver. It was a hard upbringing of Southern Baptist shame mixed with '60s and '70s free love ideologies. So, feelings, emotions, and intimacy were things best left unsaid and unexplored. We did not talk about our feelings or emotions in my house. I was given the ever so popular back then, "Stop crying or I'll give you something to cry about" from my father and a kind of Pollyanna "All is well" attitude from my mother.

They both loved me and still do, but like many of us, you cannot give what you weren't given yourself. We all do the best with what we have at every moment of every day. When we know better, we do better. But, until we know better, we do what we were taught.

Therefore, I did not have a healthy grasp on intimacy or feelings and emotions, for that matter. I ran towards the only thing that made me feel wanted and desired, even if only temporarily. Sex. Sex with as many willing girls as possible. For some reason, like most young men seem to do, I equated quantity with value. The more, the better, was all I thought.

Now, if you add in my location and the extracurricular activities that afforded me, you will soon see how my desire for intimacy and a feeling of being desired, not only lead me to a multi-decade sex addiction but also to alcoholism.

As a sixteen-year-old young man newly introduced to sex, but with less than desirable experiences in that regard. Add in the freedom of buses, subways and trains in Germany to take me and my likewise teenage angsty friends wherever we desired to go, far from the prying eyes of parents or guardians and a bit of a grey area in regard to the legal drinking ages for American kids in Germany in that time. The party was on, and we were ready and willing to embark on our adult education at full speed.

The worst part about my young partying days was my growing association of alcohol with sex. For a young man desperate for some kind of connections, hell, any kind of connection. Adding alcohol to the mix not only helped to numb the pain I was in, but it also anesthetized the feelings that sex normally would engender in a young man.

Each subsequent conquest did nothing to release the pain I was attempting to expel. On the contrary, like most addictions, it only increased the need for more and more to create any sort of satisfactory feeling.

With my sex addiction tied to a growing use and dependence on alcohol to grease the social wheels of my teenage search for acceptance and the feeling of being wanted. Soon I could scarcely separate the two from each other. Sex and alcohol went hand in hand in my mind.

I got to a point in my mid-twenties where I couldn't have sex unless I was drunk. I associated my ability to last longer and go harder in sex to the amount of alcohol I consumed. As a young man is wont to do, I then began to think that I needed alcohol for sex and would only be ready when drunk.

This also compounded the natural euphoric feeling of alcohol that tends to lead to horniness within me, to a point where I became the worst version of myself when drunk. I was a vile horny boy-man when drunk and did not like myself the next morning when I sobered up.

I say all that to say this: the first thirty years of my life were like this. Bouncing from place to place, seeking connection and a feeling of belonging in whatever way I could. Usually not in the healthiest ways. That was my generation, though and now we're grown up and have no one to blame but ourselves. We did the deeds and now have to reap the rewards.

Fortunately, like most horror stories will tell you, you just have to make it through the night and once the sun rises, you'll be safe again. I continued to battle with my addictions through the years off and on. Sometimes doing better, many times doing worse. Much of that was dependent on whether or not I was in a relationship. I tended to do better in relationships until I would ultimately sabotage them due to my lack of self-worth Devil and my Nice Guy Syndrome Devil ruining my attempted shot at a relationship.

I'd like to say that all that was a long time ago and that when I had my awakening spark moment in my late '20s, that it all stopped. But that's not how my story goes. I'm good now, but it was a long row to hoe.

As my '20s drew to a close, I went to my first meta-physical fair with my mother who came from Texas to Colorado, where I lived then, to meet Dannion Brinkley. Since we hadn't seen each other in years at that point, she invited me to come down to Denver and join her.

So at twenty-nine, I went to my first metaphysical fair and was introduced to all things metaphysical, spiritual, the Intuitives, psychics, mediums, auras, Indigo and crystal children, and the like. I had no idea who all these freaky people were and why I felt like I finally found my tribe.

Thus, the second phase of my life began and has lasted the last twenty years. I have immersed myself in everything metaphysical, self-help, personal development and so on to get me to the place I am in today. As I sit here writing this story of myself, I am struck by how perfectly everything for me was planned and orchestrated.

At my first metaphysical fair, I had my first aura picture taken, was introduced to the concept of Indigo Children and that I might be one, I met my first mentor Dannion Brinkley and was implanted with the idea that maybe I should write a book myself.

This was just the beginning of a twenty-year journey of self-exploration, self-awareness and session after session of therapy, counseling, self-improvement work and inner work. In college terms, all I need is to finish and publish my dissertation and my doctorate in metaphysical, spiritual, and personal development studies will be on its way.

Do not think that the last twenty years have been easy or pleasant. To be honest, the previous twenty years were far more fun and enjoyable in their craziness and debauchery. I was ignorant then and didn't know anything else. Ignorance is bliss and knowledge is power, but with great power comes great responsibility.

I'm convinced that most people prefer to remain ignorant and blissfully unaware, rather than to step into knowing and the responsibility that brings. I sure would like to go back myself when the going gets tough for me and just be blissfully ignorant again.

The last twenty years for me have been an expedition of failed relationships, failed business ventures, failed growth and maturation. And yet, you can't make an omelet without breaking some eggs. All these failures led me to the bottom, and from the bottom, you either dig your grave and get in it or you begin the long climb out.

I'm not sure if I'm all the way out yet or just seeing the light at the end of the tunnel up ahead. Whatever my position is, I am at a place where I can point back to my many pitfalls and failures to save you from having to recreate them for yourself.

I have spent decades being sabotaged by my own Devil, until the point that I had only two choices to make: give up or take responsibility. And, since I'm still here, I'm sure you can guess the choice I made.

After much deep inner work, soul searching, therapy, counseling, energy work, plant medicine, and in great part Internal Family System therapy, I am now sober, open to the possibility of real love and intimacy in a relationship and committed to opening my heart to love, love of myself, my whole self, and love for those who wish to love me as well.

My sobriety only came when I finally decided to take personal responsibility for my life and my Devils. The shadow work wasn't fun or pleasant, but it wasn't the Hell I thought it would be. The Devils I faced are now my superpowers. The Devils I uncovered, accepted and integrated are now my strength. My foundations that I stand on to help others in this work are cemented into the bedrock built by my Devils.

This is why I am so passionate now about Internal Family System Therapy and Parts Integration therapy. My addictions were my attempts to soothe and cover up my internal pains from my own exiled child parts. Once I met those parts with love and freed them from their self-appointed jobs as protector, manager or firefighter, I no longer felt the need to soothe or cover up my feelings.

I wasn't cursed to live in Hell by any outside Devil of evil and malice. I was blessed by parts of me that only wanted to protect me from more harm. My parts gave up their original jobs of love, compassion, creativity, joy and magic; to take on the jobs of protectors, manager and firefighters to keep me safe from the past traumas of my life that I wasn't mature enough to deal with at the time.

Now I have the opportunity to learn and master these skills by teaching what I've learned to you. True mastery only comes through teaching. The best form of teaching is embodiment and living by example. I will not profess mastery over any of my Devils yet. I will claim awareness, acceptance, understanding, utilization and integration of my Devils, my shadow side and my inner child exiles.

This is why I'm here with you now, to share my own journey and to empower you to take up the challenge of Facing the Devil in You and taking your power back.

We are all the whole expression of the Creator Source, and we have all the aspects of that source. We can use them or be used by them. The choice is yours to make, and yours to embody.

If you choose to take on this challenge, I will gladly be your guide into Hell and back. Saddle up, pardners, into the Inferno we go and out the other side like the Phoenix, reborn from your own inner fire.

I am here to help as a loving witness to your own inner children who are patiently waiting for you to acknowledge them, reparent them, and reintegrate them into the whole of you. I am your guide, not because I'm better than or know more than you. No, I am your guide because I can relate to you from my own past experience and in so doing, hopefully save you a lot of time, pain, and energy in the process.

I do not and cannot judge you or anyone else for their pasts of pain, addiction, or trauma. I've lived too many lifetimes, being the worst of the worst to have any sort of judgment towards another person on their spiritual path.

I've been the worst, so I can understand the worst. I'm working toward the best version of myself and would like to invite you along with me. Let's explore these inner Devils together and turn them into our inner strengths.

Chapter One

WHO AND WHAT IS THE DEVIL?

I f you picked up this book hoping to learn more about "The Devil," the modern conception of Evil, or were just struck by the title and became curious; you will get something out of this work, but, I imagine, not what you were expecting.

Let us begin with the concept of the Devil...

Instead of me attempting to wax poetically about this concept. I will instead turn to the internet to fill you in on what is currently out there on Who and What the Devil is...

Excerpt from Wikipedia:

A devil is the personification of evil as it is conceived in various cultures and religious traditions.[1] It is seen as the objectification of a hostile and destructive force.[2] Jeffrey Burton Russell states that the different conceptions of the devil can be summed up as 1) a principle of evil independent from God, 2) an aspect of God, 3) a created being turning evil (a fallen angel), and 4) a symbol of human evil.[3]:23

Each tradition, culture, and religion with a devil in its mythos offers a different lens on manifestations of evil.[4] The history of these perspectives intertwines with theology, mythology, psychiatry, art, and literature, developing independently within each of the traditions.[5] It occurs historically in many contexts and cultures, and is given many different names—Satan, Lucifer, Beelzebub, Mephistopheles, Iblis—and attributes: it is portrayed as blue, black, or red; it is portrayed as having horns on its head, and without horns, and so on.[6][7]

Etymology

The Modern English word devil derives from the Middle English devel, from the Old English dēofol, that in turn represents an early Germanic borrowing of the Latin diabolus. This in turn was borrowed from the Greek διάβολος diábolos, "slanderer,"[8] from διαβάλλειν diabállein, "to slander" from διά diá, "across, through" and βάλλειν bállein, "to hurl," probably akin to the Sanskrit gurate, "he lifts up."[9]

Now, that should be clear as mud… As my dad was wont to say.

I'm sure you do get an idea of what most modern people have been taught or think about the concept of a Devil.

Here is where I will deviate from what we traditionally have been told, taught or thought about this Devilish concept.

In my experience and opinion, as well and that of the Illustrious Napoleon Hill of *Think and Grow Rich* and *Outwitting the Devil* fame, "The Devil" is nothing more or less than the negative force in the universe. Whether you want to equate that force with the weak electromagnetic forces in particle physics, the trough of the wave function in vibrational frequencies, or the interactions of dark to light.

In any case, what you'll come to find out when you take away all the personal belief systems that we've been taught about this "red-horned Devil conspiring to steal our souls," you'll see that this force is just the balancing force to the positive and light sides of the universe.

Without Darkness, light has no meaning. Without light, darkness is meaningless. Without cold, hot means nothing. Without Negative, Positive is a non-sequitur.

The "DEVIL" in other words is the necessary balancing force of the universe and that which gives our reality the depth and meaning that we need to have to have an experience of reality.

You cannot know light without the contrast of dark. You cannot know love without the contrast of fear. You cannot know your perception of good without your perception of Bad or Evil. Each aspect of creation is dependent on the other for its very existence. You cannot know one without the other.

Now I will take you down a little rabbit hole of my own and tell you about my thoughts on the matter. Take what resonates and save the rest for later growth.

What we all know as the Creator, the Source of all that is, what many call GOD, is this. God, the Creator, the Source can easily be defined in the exact same way that we define energy at its most basic level, i.e., always was, always will be. Cannot be created or destroyed. It moves into form, through form and out of form. *This is also known as the First Law of Thermodynamics*.

God can best be described as "ALL THAT IS," meaning that everything in this Universe of our shared collective consciousness is, always has been, and always will be God.

Therefore, if God is "All that is," then God is the light and the dark, the strong and the weak, the sun and the moon, the birth and the death, the Alpha and Omega, the good and the evil, the positive and the negative, the wanted and unwanted. God is all that is and the only thing the God isn't, is nothing. Because, by its very definition, Nothing or No-Thing, doesn't exist. And, that which doesn't exist, cannot, by definition, exist. There is no such thing as nonexistence and therefore nothing outside of God.

I will utilize Occam's Razor, which states: All things being equal, the simplest answer tends to be the right one. And, following that logic, it would seem reasonable to state that the anthropomorphized character we call the Devil, is just another piece of God that is necessary for this whole big machine to work.

I recently had an "aha" moment at a conference where the subject of Napoleon Hill's book *Outwitting the Devil* came up and thought to myself; "What if the 'Devil' was just God's drill instructor or trainer of divinity?"

I mean, think about it. There are so many humans alive today who have gone to the depths of despair, their own private Hell, if you will, and came out the holiest of the holies and most inspired, of the inspired to live a righteous life of servitude to the rest of humanity.

I'm not saying that this is a must for all of us to Dance with the Devil in order to become the best version of ourselves, but I do believe that without a healthy respect for and understanding of our darkest depths and potential there is really no way for us to be able to step into our fullest authentic self. As the old saying goes, "It is better to be a Warrior in the garden, than a Gardener in a War." Or to paraphrase a quote from Jordan Peterson, "A good man is a very dangerous man who has that danger under control."

The Devil in each of us is our capacity for fear, negativity, selfishness, arrogance, greed, narcissism, projection, anger, hate, fury, and so on. However, I am of the belief that it isn't our capacity for these things that is the issue, but our resistance to these capacities. You cannot truly fulfill your potential when you are denying half of yourself.

Until we face and come to an understanding with the "Devil" within us, we cannot be truly free to shine our unique gifts into the world.

One way I have always found to accept and better integrate what most would call the "Bad" or "Negative" side of ourselves is to realize that we are holistic beings made of all parts of the ALL. We are equally light and dark, loving and hateful, big and small, happy and sad, ignorant and knowledgeable, etc.

I'll again point to Occam's Razor to illustrate this point. All things being equal, the simplest answer is usually the correct one. Therefore, if we are made up of all parts of the ALL, then we are equally all things. However you choose to define it, we are made up of portions of all of the ALL and capable of infinite potential. We are a piece of that one Singularity that we call GOD, INFINITY, THE ALL THAT IS, THE UNIVERSE, and so on.

Now that we can theorize and hypothesize about our wholeness and holisticness, we can begin to see that what we are fighting against and afraid of is just a part of ourselves we are ignorant of, and what we don't understand, we tend to fear. The idea of a dualistic nature instead of a holistic one is part and parcel of all the problems we as humans have in our unique creation of life.

You are a whole being full of all parts of the ALL. You are capable of the greatest greatness and the lowest lowness. It is just a matter of mindset and choice in every moment. However, you cannot choose when you are not allowing all of you into the equation.

Not acknowledging or allowing all parts of you to exist within and inhabit your consciousness is a denial of critical parts of your nature that are needed to live a whole and balanced life. Without an awareness and utilization of all parts of you, you are missing critical ingredients and thereby critical information in your decision-making process.

Many, if not most, of us would rather ignore and deny those parts of ourselves that we "Don't Like," but it is within those parts that our power lies. You cannot live on light alone. You must have darkness within which to rest and recharge.

You cannot know Light without also knowing Darkness. This is the wholeness of God and of Life.

The biggest thing to keep in mind as we delve into the topic of the Devil in You is this: Where your attention goes, energy flows. What you put your mind on and think about most often is what you create in your unique experience of life. If your main focus is on evil, negativity, bad luck, judgment, criticism, and all that you do not prefer in the world, you will have a realistic experience of what we have termed the Devil in our society.

Your beliefs, thoughts and attitude make up how you experience the world around you and can turn life into Heaven on Earth, or just as easily, Hell on Earth.

Many of my most rigorously religious acquaintances experience far more of the Devil than they do of the Christ Consciousness side of life, due to how they think and how they use their focus. By being so focused on fighting the Devil and Evil, they create the experience of the Devil working Evil in their lives and become a victim of Evil by their constant focus and creation of that experience.

So many of those preaching the blessings of Jesus/ Yeshua, to the world are so focused on fighting against Evil that they experience a far more Devilish life than a Loving and Blessed life.

You are the chooser and creator of your unique experience and if you choose to use your powerful focus on fighting evil, then that is what you will create and experience in your life.

On the other hand, if you choose to focus on the good, love and light in the world, then that is what you will create and experience in your life.

The infinite love and blessings of the creator may look like apathy to some, but in truth is the greatest expression of unconditional love in creation, because we are allowed to create and experience anything we desire in each lifetime for the experience and learning we gain from it.

God loves you so much that he/she is willing to allow you to create anything you desire for as long as you wish until you gain enough experience and wisdom to come back to the light of love and connection.

That is why I say that the Devil in You is your greatest teacher and friend, because it will punish you and keep you in whatever Hell you choose, until you learn your lesson and choose the Love of your Creator again.

As an eternal being of light and love that cannot die, you are allowed to experience anything you wish for as long as you wish too. And you are allowed to change your mind whenever you are ready to for a new experience of creation.

Your Devil is totally your creation and responsibility. Which is a wonderful thing, because it means you are in control of it and can choose to change your mind and your experience NOW.

Chapter Two

DEVIL, SHADOW OR DEMON

I use the term "DEVIL" because of the effect that term elicits in most people. This concept is not about an evil entity committed to stealing your soul, but more about the natural negative side of life that we all deal with. However, for those of you who have a religious upbringing and who cannot abide by the term of the "DEVIL" being a part of you, then we can easily substitute the word "DEVIL" with "SHADOW."

I believe even my very religious friends can accept that we all have a shadow side and that we all have aspects that we wish to understand better and utilize in a more positive way. For you I have added this chapter about "The Shadow." Now you can mentally substitute the term "DEVIL" for the term "SHADOW."

THE CONCEPT OF THE SHADOW

The concept of the Shadow, a term popularized by psychologist Carl Jung, represents the parts of ourselves that we often choose to ignore or suppress. It encompasses our fears, insecurities, and the traits we deem undesirable. For many individuals, especially those in generations X, Y, and Z, the idea of confronting these hidden aspects can seem daunting. Yet, embracing the shadow is a crucial step in the journey of self-discovery and personal growth. By acknowledging our shadow, we can unlock a deeper understanding of ourselves, leading to greater authenticity and purpose in our lives.

One of the most inspiring facets of shadow work is its potential for transformation. When we begin to explore our shadow, we will uncover hidden talents, strengths, and passions that we've overlooked or hidden due to our self-judgment. These revelations can be empowering, prompting us to pursue paths that resonate more deeply with our true selves. For example, a young adult who has always been told or believes they must pursue a traditional career might discover a passion for art or music that has been buried under layers of societal expectation. Embracing this shadow aspect can propel them toward a fulfilling career that aligns with their authentic interests and values.

The process of integrating the shadow is not merely about acknowledging our flaws; it's also about fostering compassion towards ourselves. In a world that often emphasizes perfectionism, learning to accept our imperfections can be revolutionary. This self-compassion allows us to free ourselves from the shackles of self-judgment and shame, enabling a more profound connection with our inner selves. As we learn to love and accept our shadow, we cultivate resilience and openness, making room for personal growth and transformation that can inspire those around us.

Furthermore, the journey into the shadow can enhance our relationships with others. When we embrace our own darkness, we become more empathetic and understanding of the struggles faced by those around us. This shared vulnerability can lead to deeper connections and more meaningful interactions. In a time when many individuals are striving for authenticity in their relationships, recognizing and embracing our shadows can create a safe space for others to do the same. This mutual acceptance fosters a community where growth, healing, and support flourish.

Ultimately, embracing the concept of the shadow is a courageous act of self-love and acceptance. It invites us to look beyond the surface and engage with the complexities of our identity. As we navigate the challenges of modern life, especially within the dynamics of our interconnected generations, acknowledging our shadow becomes not just a personal endeavor but a collective movement towards healing and authenticity. By embarking on this journey together, we can redefine our understanding of self-discovery and empower each other to live fuller, more meaningful lives.

DEMONS:

In addition to the ideas of a Devil or the Shadow, many associate the term Demon with an evil entity committed to your demise. Demons are associated with the Devil as his minions of evil and who entice humans into giving up their souls.

Many cultures place Demons alongside their versions of the Devil and treat them accordingly. One is just a different version of the other. There is little to no distinction between the two. They are here to damn you and steal your soul to take to the Devil.

Once again, let's take a little trip down the rabbit hole of language and etymology to discover the true origins of the concept of Demons.

The term "demon" originally referred to a spirit or divine power in Ancient Greek (daimōn), and didn't carry a negative connotation. Over time, through translations of the Hebrew Bible and the influence of Semitic mythology, the word began to be associated with evil or malevolent entities. While the word "demon" can be used to describe a person with great energy or skill, it's more commonly understood as a term for a devil, evil spirit, or a person regarded as evil. The negative association with bad emotions or "demons" is a more recent and metaphorical interpretation.

Here's a more detailed breakdown:

Ancient Greek (daimōn):

This term originally meant a spirit, divine power, or lesser god, sometimes including the souls of the dead. It was seen as a guiding spirit or tutelary deity, associated with one's fortune or destiny.

Septuagint Translation:

The translation of the Hebrew Bible into Greek (Septuagint) introduced the term "daemon" with negative connotations, influenced by Semitic mythology.

Christian Context:

In Christian belief, "demon" became associated with evil spirits, devils, or fiends, often seen as supernatural beings that could tempt or influence humans.

Metaphorical Use:

The concept of "demons" as internal, negative emotions or influences is a more recent and figurative usage. It's used to describe intense passions like jealousy, anger, or other negative emotions that seem to control a person.

Let's focus on the last paragraph here and the association of Demons with Bad emotions.

As I pointed out earlier, the Devil is just the anthropomorphized image of what we consider negativity. Similarly, Demons are the anthropomorphized images of our negative or "BAD" emotions.

Not to say that there aren't entities in the multi-dimensional multiverse that can and do feed off of Human energy fields and life force. Everyone has to eat, and if you are offering yourself up to negative emotions and feelings, something will take advantage.

However, when you realize that Devilish or Demonic forces can only attach to you or feed off you when you are in the depths of negative emotions, you can then understand your own power to deny these entities a meal.

When we place these concepts into the proper context, we can see that we are the ones in control and in power here. Only by giving into our basest instincts and feelings do we open up to these negative entities.

This is why I put that quote from Bashar in the opening page of the book. Demons are not outside entities feeding off you against your will, but merely parts of you that you allow to access too, by not understanding your own emotional state and power.

Your negative emotions create the negative world you envision. You are the creator, and you are the master of your reality. Yet, when you are taught to believe in negative evil entities who force evil upon you against your will, you create just that. Your power lies in your awareness. When you realize this, you will see all the forces vying for your attention to dictate what you experience and keep you under their control.

You have the power to control your emotions through proper use of your mind, focus, and attention. When you choose to see positive instead of negative and take the time needed to reprogram your mind, you will see this change reflected in your experienced reality.

Demons are nothing more than negative emotions given freedom to run amok. Just like your kids will tear the house down without proper supervision, so too will your negative emotions tear down your proverbial house when left unsupervised.

How many times have you seen this play out in your own life? You wake up on the wrong side of the bed and think you are a victim of your mood, so you do nothing to change it, and your day goes from bad to worse. This is how we create our unique realities through thought, belief, and emotion.

Had you woken up on the wrong side of the bed, acknowledged it, and decided to change your emotional state, you would have had a far different day indeed.

We are taught to believe we are the victims of life, circumstance and chance, but we are nothing of the sort. We are the commanders and captains of our own ships, and we steer our experiences as we see fit. The power to direct your life, circumstances, and emotions is right between your ears. You've just been taught and led to believe that you have no control over the Demons of the world.

Your Demons are yours to set loose or control as you see fit. You decide. Not them. They have no power over you except what you give them to use.

Do not believe that you have no control over your emotions and must suffer them to exist as they are. You are the control. You are the power. You are the decider of your emotional state.

How often have you been in a mood and your loved ones do their best to help you out of it, but you aren't willing to shift? It's your pity party and you'll cry if you want to.

I get it, we've all been there. Alternatively, we've also all been on the other side, attempting to cheer up another who just isn't having it. They want to stay stuck and miserable and nothing you can do or say will get them out of it until they choose to.

Your Demons, like your Devils and your Shadows are yours to control or yours to be controlled by. You have the power to acquiesce to these negative emotions and thereby create a negative experience in your personal reality. Or you can choose to control your emotional state and create one you would prefer to experience today.

I do understand that if you have been in the depths of despair and can see no way out at this moment, these words can sound a little bit too good to be true and farfetched. I understand and I've been there. It is hard to see past your present state when you're deep in it. Just know that you have the power to change it when you are ready to.

Demons cannot control you without your permission and your willingness to play along. You are the actor in your play and the director and set designer and makeup artist and wardrobe designer and the audience. You pick it all and experience what you choose.

Granted, some of our decisions are made by us prior to arriving here in this body here on Earth. Many of us chose seemingly awful lives to live prior to incarnation and we don't remember why.

Here is the gist of your spiritual choices that you've forgotten you made.

You, the real you, the eternal spiritual being you, who wants to help the Creator expand in experiencing all that is through us, decided for the purpose of having the experience and the lessons therein, to pick your unique circumstances of life. Your parents, your environment, your country, your religious affiliations, your sex, your preferences and your traumas. You chose all of it to have the unique experience of expression you are having now.

You are the chooser, the experiencer, the author and the reader of your story.

In my first two books, *It's Not Your Life, It's You*, books one and two, I delve fully into this topic of choice and responsibility for your life choices. You have no one to blame but yourself for the predicament you're in. And since you chose it, you have all the power to un-choose it and change it as you see fit.

However, keep in mind that you chose it for a reason and the fact that you can't remember the reason, doesn't mean you should just throw the baby out with the bath water until you first have some idea of why you chose these set of circumstances to live through.

Many people ask me things like: If I'm unable to deal with my Demons and can't improve my situation, can I just check out of this life? ... And the answer is: Yes, you can come and go as you please. However, if you choose to leave life before you are done with your current lesson and learning, you will come back to repeat it. You will keep coming back as many times as you need to learn the lesson you chose to learn.

So, to put it bluntly, there is nothing wrong with suicide or leaving the body early from a spiritual standpoint. You are an eternal spiritual being having thousands of life adventures. Except that, if you quit playing before your game is up, you will be back to play it again.

You are better off figuring out why you chose these Demons and what you are trying to learn from them. Once you figure out your why for this life experience, you will no longer want to leave early. More often than not, when someone discovers why they chose these life circumstances, they feel empowered and encouraged to finish the game.

Nothing in life has any intrinsic meaning, which means you give everything in life all the meaning that it has for you. You chose this life, and you choose what it means. You are not a victim of a cruel God or the Vicissitudes of Fate. You just forgot the game you chose to play, and your Demons are just showing you the way back.

Face your Devils, face your shadows, face your Demons and let them show you why you are here and what you chose as the purpose and lesson for this life. Everything is connected and leads you back to God. You just have to look with an open mind and heart to see the magical Choose Your Own Adventure game you chose to play.

Now, to beat this dead Demon some more. Look into your emotions, especially the negative ones, to find out where they are leading you. A negative emotion is just a road sign towards what you prefer to experience. Follow your emotional signs back to your innate power of creation and to the purpose you chose for this incarnational experience.

In my work as a coach, I come across so many who have a hard time seeing their whole selves because they refuse to look at, acknowledge and integrate their negative emotions in any way. It is far too common these days for people to outright ignore and deny any "Negative" part of them in a vain attempt to be perfect or in an attempt to play perfect.

Without an honest acknowledgement and assessment of one's less than desirable traits, you become a victim and slave to those emotions. Any emotion left unacknowledged and undealt with becomes the Demon running and ruining your life.

You have never been a victim to the world around you, except when you consciously or unconsciously agree to play along with the emotions running. The path to freedom is unapologetic and authentic acknowledgement of every part of ourselves, especially the "Negative" parts.

We, as humans, cannot hope to master ourselves without acknowledging, accepting, investigating, integrating, understanding and utilizing those very negative emotions we've run from for so long. There really is no such thing as a negative or "Bad" emotion. Emotions are just "Energy in Motion." It's all just energy and energy is neither good nor bad. It just is.

Acknowledgment of our emotions is just the first step to gain your power back from them and through them. Since emotions are just energy in motion, the act of denying and rejecting our own emotions causes a blockage of that energy. That blockage then turns stagnant and dark, like a stagnant pool of water. All sorts of nasty things begin to grow in and flourish in that stagnant energy. These stagnant pools of energy within each of us become our diseases, addictions and sources of self-sabotage.

Energy must be allowed to flow. Just like water, if it isn't allowed to flow and remain active, it becomes stagnant and sickly. This stagnant and sick energy becomes blockages which turn into all sorts of physical issues within us.

This philosophy is the basis for many Eastern health techniques, like Reiki, Qui Gong, Tai Chi, etc. All these techniques are designed to move energy. When we move our bodies, we are moving energy. When we consciously direct energy to flow to remove blockages, we generate healing in our bodies.

A study of the chakra system, meridian system and nervous/energetic systems of the body will show you the pathways of energy within us that need to flow, but are constantly being blocked due to immobility, poor diet, poor exercise and first and foremost, blocked emotions from our past. This is why acknowledging and releasing those blocked emotions from our past is so vital to health, wealth and success in life. You cannot raise your vibration with a blocked energetic system.

To reach the higher vibrational fields that we all need to be the best versions of ourselves in this life starts with diving deep into those black pools of stagnant emotional energy that you buried in your past as a child. You're an adult now and have all the tools and resources you need to not only heal those past emotional traumas, but to also turn them into your superpowers.

You are not under attack from a devilish demon sent from Hell. You are the victim of your unacknowledged and unhealed inner child wounds. You are not the victim, but the master of those demonic forces within you. Like the Mogwai fed after midnight will turn into a Gremlin, your suppressed past emotions will turn into your Demons if not accepted and released by you.

In my own personal example, I lived with sex addiction and alcoholism for three decades and felt in every way the victim to these issues. That was until I began my inner work and got right down into the depths of my inner child's traumas. My inner child traumas came from well-meaning parents, who just passed down the same things they received from their parents. My younger self didn't have the awareness, maturity or awareness to be able to deal with those situations at those times.

Now that I am older and more experienced, it is very easy for me to acknowledge, understand, and integrate those past childhood traumas that I couldn't deal with, much less understand, when I was a child. I now have the honor and responsibility to re-raise my inner child-self and to heal what I was once unaware of as trauma and stagnant emotional energy.

The Demons you believe you are battling within you are nothing more than an exiled inner child part of you who has gotten out of control attempting to release the stagnant energy from the past experiences that originally created the trauma. You now have the power and awareness to lovingly bring your exiled child part back into the fold of the greater whole of you.

The simple beauty of acknowledging and accepting that traumatized inner child part of you is a magical and loving experience. Just like the heart-opening joy we feel when a loving little child hugs us and melts our hearts, this is the same experience you can have within yourself as you release those lost and lonely exiled inner child parts of yourself and bring them back home to you.

Whatever your addiction, coping mechanism or anxiety may seem to be, they are all just stuck energies within you begging for release. Set yourself and your Demons free. You can do it and you should do it, because the world needs all of you in your best version to fulfill your purpose here on the planet.

We all need you and love you, even if we've never met or will never meet. We are all in this together and need each other at our individual best. The Golden Age of love and light starts within each of us here on the planet. As we heal and gain the higher vibration of love and light, we act as a beacon and example for others to do the same.

The work is not "Out There," it is "In Here," in you, in your heart, mind and body. You are the one you've been waiting for; you have the power to create the life of your dreams. You just need to free your energy and free the power inside you.

Chapter Three

THE BIG BANG

For those of my readers of the more scientific bent, I wanted to add a chapter about the Big Bang to help illustrate the oneness of all things and how I can proclaim that God and the Devil are one entity and that we have both dark and light within each of us, as it was meant to be.

Many of you are familiar with the Big Bang Theory of the creation of the Universe. This is a widely accepted theory in science and the world today. No one is 100% sure of its accuracy, but it's the best explanation we've come up with so far as to how we came into being. I'm going to take this concept in a different direction than most of you have previously considered, and hopefully, in doing so, will be able to bring this and the concept of oneness or we are all one into a nice package for you.

This concept also helps to illustrate how the concept of dualism is false, and the Theory of Oneness is actually more correct. Everything began as a singularity, a oneness, if you will, which means that everything we see, and experience is just a part of that oneness or singularity. Just as a drop in the ocean isn't the ocean, but the ocean is the drop and infinite other drops, can illustrate the point of oneness.

However, I am aware that we are creator beings, who create our personal realities through our thoughts and belief systems. Depending on your unique perspective, I acknowledge that it can be very difficult to address the concept of oneness when everything you have been taught and believe is derived from a belief in separation and duality. That is why I am adding this chapter on the BIG BANG to help illustrate in a Scientific way how we all derive from oneness and thereby are intrinsically ONE.

Here is the Big Bang Theory as defined on Big-Bang-Theory.com:

> *{Big Bang Theory — The Premise*
> *The Big Bang theory is an effort to explain what happened at the very beginning of our universe. Discoveries in astronomy and physics have shown beyond a reasonable doubt that our universe did in fact have a beginning. Prior to that moment there was nothing; during and after that moment there was something: our universe. The big bang theory is an effort to explain what happened during and after that moment.*

According to the standard theory, our universe sprang into existence as "singularity" around 13.7 billion years ago. What is a "singularity" and where does it come from? Well, to be honest, we don't know for sure. Singularities are zones which defy our current understanding of physics. They are thought to exist at the core of "black holes." Black holes are areas of intense gravitational pressure. The pressure is thought to be so intense that finite matter is actually squished into infinite density (a mathematical concept which truly boggles the mind). These zones of infinite density are called "singularities." Our universe is thought to have begun as an infinitesimally small, infinitely hot, infinitely dense, something - a singularity. Where did it come from? We don't know. Why did it appear? We don't know.

After its initial appearance, it apparently inflated (the "Big Bang"), expanded and cooled, going from very, very small and very, very hot, to the size and temperature of our current universe. It continues to expand and cool to this day and we are inside of it: incredible creatures living on a unique planet, circling a beautiful star clustered together with several hundred billion other stars in a galaxy soaring through the cosmos, all of which is inside of an expanding universe that began as an infinitesimal singularity which appeared out of nowhere for reasons unknown. This is the Big Bang theory.}

Many scientists, including Albert Einstein, believe that the natural rhythm of the universe is to expand outward from the initial moment of creation, which we are still experiencing now, and then to contract back in on itself. Then back out and back in again, like a breath in and out of the universal body, if you will.

Now, I know nothing about the contraction phase, but having seen much of the same cycle here on our planet of heating and cooling, growth and death, expansion and contraction, I can honestly say that if the microcosm has any relation to the macrocosm, then logically speaking, this is probably true. What does that have to do with us on this planet today… No idea! It is interesting to think about, though, and it brings a lot of concepts into a new light to consider.

Have you noticed any expansions and contractions in your life? Any ups and downs to speak of? Any good days or bad days? Are you still breathing?

These are simple examples of the cyclical nature of our lives, world, and the universe. If we have enough expanded awareness, we can learn much about the whole from the pieces or the macrocosm from the microcosm. And, in all things and in all ways, life and experience are cyclical.

Let's look at the world we're living in today. The beginning of the 21st century. The beginning of the Age of Aquarius. The time prophesied by the Mayans to be the Ending of the Mayan calendar. Have you heard of the Cosmic Convergence that happened in 1987? Did you see the alignment of the planets at the beginning of 2025?

Unlike any other time in our personal history, this time is a time of change and awakening here on this planet and in the universe at large. As our ET brothers and sisters are telling us, this is where it's all happening now. All eyes are on Earth and what we'll do in the next hundred years.

As with the beginning of a cycle there is an end. We are at the end of the Kali yuga, the great night and entering into a new day. However, these are cosmic cycles and take a lot longer than our 24-hour-day experience.

Here is an excerpt from google about the Kali Yuga:

In Hinduism, Kali Yuga is the fourth and current age in the cycle of yugas (ages) and is often referred to as the "Age of Darkness" or the "Dark Age." It is characterized by a decline in morality, spirituality, and righteousness, with a focus on materialism and a diminishing reverence for dharma (righteousness).

Here's a more detailed explanation:

Cycle of Yugas:

Hinduism believes in a cyclical nature of time, with four yugas (or ages) comprising a cycle: Satya Yuga (Age of Truth), Treta Yuga, Dvapara Yuga, and Kali Yuga.

Characteristics of Kali Yuga:

Kali Yuga is marked by a decrease in virtues like truth, righteousness, and spiritual awareness. People are believed to be more concerned with material possessions and pleasures, leading to a decline in spiritual practices and knowledge.

Belief in the Future:

Some Hindu beliefs suggest that Kali Yuga will eventually end with the arrival of Kalki, the tenth avatar of Vishnu, who will usher in a new Satya Yuga.

Significance of Kali Yuga:

While often depicted as a negative period, Kali Yuga is also seen as an opportunity for spiritual growth and liberation, as the hardships and challenges of the age can encourage individuals to seek enlightenment and detachment from material desires.

As you can see, the Kali Yuga perfectly depicts our current times on the planet. We have gone just about as far as we can go into separation, materialism, and greed. We're all feeling the pull back into unity and wholeness.

This Planetary Unity and the wholeness of humanity starts with you, inside yourself. You are the first step towards planetary unification. We cannot unite as a people if each person is at war within themselves. Your Kali Yuga or Age of Darkness is also coming to an end, and you are entering your own personal new day.

Your new day begins with you doing your personal inner work of facing your Devil, your shadow and reintegrating them into wholeness within you. As above, so below, illustrates why we're all feeling the pull back into personal oneness and why you picked up this book in the first place. There are no accidents, and you aren't reading these words by chance. We are coming together now to continue down the path of awakening and into the next Golden Age of humanity.

We're in this together and can support one another by sharing our stories, our traumas, our dark nights of the soul, and our own Devils with one another. Power comes from sharing together and unity comes from seeing ourselves in others.

The Big Bang may have been the beginning of our universal story, but Facing the Devil in You is the beginning of our shared stories of oneness and unity on our way into the next Golden Age of Light, Love, and Peace.

The beginning of the universe is a mystery wrapped in a paradox, topped with an enigma. Yet, I truly believe that even though we may never know the whole story in our finite physical bodies, we can get a general picture of the workings of the universe and in that way empower ourselves with the wisdom of the ages and the magic of our uniqueness.

You are a unique expression of the creator, The All that is, God. There is no one else in the whole universe that is, can, or will be you. No one and nothing can ever replace you in any way, shape, or form. You are a beautiful and unique snowflake within the avalanche of consciousness that is the awakening of humanity. That is why you're reading this book.

But here is the big "but" that creates the paradox within which we all exist and live. You, me, we are all one. Have you heard of this before? We are all one… Now, how can we all be one and unique at the same time? Well, I'm happy you asked! I have an answer for you to ponder and consider which could bring a new perspective to all things in your life.

If you consider the Big Bang Theory as defined previously, you remember that the universe started as a singularity. We are still working the bugs out on understanding singularities, but we know each black hole has one at its center… Or at least we think they do. Regardless of the truth, that particular piece of information we are going to assume is true for the sake of this train of thought.

Everything started out as a singularity. Singularities are very dense hot balls of matter, anti-matter and pretty much everything else. Matter cannot escape a black hole or singularity. Anything that comes too close is sucked into it and compressed. This is the basic scientific description of singularity. I'd like to offer a similar but different definition to further my purposes here.

A spiritual singularity, as I like to call it, is the place where all things begin as one. The Creator, Is, God, All That IS would be the name we use for this singularity. The place from which all awareness and consciousness come from is this sort of singularity. In terms of this singularity, the one consciousness is all things and no-thing. It is everywhere at once and nowhere at all.

Many philosophical scholars have been playing with this idea of oneness in a myriad of ways since the beginning of recorded history. We can come close to a sense of this, but I doubt we will ever be able to get a real handle on such a nebulous concept as oneness in a world of infinite variations and a multitude of dimensional realities.

However, I believe that the Big Bang Theory is a good place to start when it is applied in this way. We, as pure consciousness, were sitting in our black hole, being all things and no-things while being everywhere and nowhere all in the same instant of no-time in which we existed. Then a decision was made that we wanted to experience our oneness in a multitude of different ways and BOOM! In that instant, our one-dimensional all that is existence fragmented into an unlimited array of dimensions, unique expressions, and possibilities.

We went from one dimension to at least eleven and more like into an unlimited number of possible dimensional realities in which to express, experience and just be in. Because infinity and eternity are really big and long, and we had to find something to do with our time, as it were.

Also, for there to be an experience of anything, there has to be more than one dimension because each dimension gives depth, and in so doing, it gives something to reference to and from. An example would be a drawing on a piece of paper. The paper is two-dimensional, and the drawing is only distinguishable on the paper because of the two-dimensional reality. However, without the third dimension of reality, we would not be able to perceive the paper or the drawing on it.

You see, you can only perceive all the dimensions within or, for lack of a better term, below your own dimension of perspective or reality. Without at least a fourth-dimensional consciousness, you would not be able to be aware of the three-dimensional construct before you. Just as you need seven reference points in space to plot a destination, the six points that define your destination and the one point that defines your starting point, you also need at least one more dimensional reality of awareness to perceive the realities within.

I know it seems complicated, but if you take a piece of paper and place it flat on the table, you can get a feel for this by seeing the paper as a plane or one dimension. Now fold the paper at a right angle, and you have a representation of two dimensions. Create another right-angle fold, and you have the representation of a third dimension. Now, if you realize that if you were not in a higher dimension of awareness, you would not be able to recognize this little experiment. Simply because if you were just a point in space or a one-dimensional reality, you would have no point of reference to distinguish between here and there or up from down. There would be no special awareness at all. But once you add in more dimensions, you begin to have reference points and can establish a framework for experience.

Whew!! Ok, now that we've gotten through that we can move forward and gain something from this that is beneficial to this conversation.

Since we all came from a singularity of all this is we, by definition, are all one. We are all part of the same source, and that is why we can say, know, and believe that we are all one. We all sprang forth from the same fount of existence, and in essence, we are the same being expressing itself in an unlimited number of ways. And, if you just asked the age-old universal question, "Why?," well, all I can tell you is, because we could and because we needed something to do. Eternity is boring if you don't find something to do.

Chapter Four

CYCLES OF LIFE

A s with all things in our universe of experience, the only constant is change. And all that change comes in cycles. As with the seasons of nature, we have seasons and cycles of life. From Birth to Death and back again, we are an ever evolving being of creation.

I am of the opinion that it is easier and more beneficial to have an awareness of the cycles of life so that we may take advantage of life's constant change, instead of being a victim to it.

As we are exploring the concept of our own personal Devil, we ought to explore life's changes, because many of us have attributed life's changes to the Devil in our attempt to resist and rebuke the natural life cycles we're all a part of. The Devil didn't do it, and you are not a victim of evil or bad luck. You chose to have this experience of the finite to give some contrast to your true nature of infinite beingness.

Just as the night gives the day meaning, the finite gives infinity meaning. The cycles of your life give your life meaning and importance. It is simply our lack of awareness of these cycles that cause us to resist and refute that which is nature and important for our life experiences to have substance and meaning.

There are cycles to life that we go through in many different variations and varied differences from our inception to our death and around again. One way to categorize these cycles is to look at them through the phases of learning. Even though these phases were constructed as a guide to explain how a person learns something, they also apply very nicely to life in its varied phases, experiences, and expressions.

Phase One is when you begin to learn something. You start in the first phase, Unconscious Incompetence, where you don't know that you don't know. There is something out there that you haven't heard of and has never come into your experience thus far. So, you don't even know that you don't know about it.

Phase Two starts when you've been introduced to this new thing and it is called Conscious Incompetence, now you know that you don't know. This is the point where you decide whether you want to learn about this new thing or not. You've been introduced to it, you know you know nothing about it and you can now decide whether you'd like to proceed on to the next steps of learning.

Phase three is Conscious Competence. This is when you've learned something new, and you have to think about it or remain conscious of it. It's like learning a new skill like tying a tie or your shoes. You must think about what you are doing to get from here to there or to get the desired result.

Phase Four happens after you've been in the Conscious Competence phase for long enough that you train your mind and body into Unconscious Competence. This is the phase where you do things without having to think about it. You can get home or to work without even thinking about it, it's just natural. You tie your shoes without thinking about it now, but the first time you had to memorize how to do it. You went through all the phases and now you are unconsciously competent at tying your shoes and many other daily tasks.

So, to recap:

Phase One – Unconscious Incompetence

You don't know that you don't know.

Phase Two – Conscious Incompetence

You know that you don't know.

Phase Three – Conscious Competence

You are learning something new and have to think about it.

Phase Four – Unconscious Competence

You have habitualzed the task and no longer have to think about it to complete it.

What I find the most interesting about these phases as they relate to people in their everyday lives is that they can be applied to the microcosm of the day-to-day as well as to the macrocosm of the whole life experience. You go through all these phases every time you go somewhere new. Every time you have a new experience, you go through these phases. Sometimes, you even go through these phases several times with the same person or situation, these are normally called relationships, and you can go through all four stages several times in one day.

The reason I bring up these learning cycles here after a chapter entitled The Big Bang is to illustrate the cyclical nature of all things, including you and me. The universe is no different, and as we grow and learn, so too does the universe. We expand and contract like the tides, and if you are very clever and pay attention to all the signs in your life, you can predict and anticipate these cycles in your life. Just like the Mayans were able to create a calendar that spanned 5,000 years to the Galactic alignment by studying the cycles of the planets and stars, so too can you learn to become aware of your own personal cycles of life.

I find it very empowering, when going through my phases of life, to keep in mind what phase I'm in, if I can. It lets me know that I am constantly moving forward and making progress in my life, whether it looks like it on the outside or not. Movement and change are the only constants in the universe. And these movements and changes follow a cyclical pattern that we can easily see if we only have the open-minded awareness to do so.

Another aspect of the Cycles of Life is the Cycles of Lives and how we go from one cycle to the next from lifetime to lifetime as we learn and grow. There are cycles of Human Spiritual evolution as well from lifetime to lifetime. I've found this awareness very helpful when interacting with other humans while I'm doing my work.

When you are aware of the cycles of learning and awareness for humans on their spiritual educational journey from life to life, you can more easily accept where they are on their spiritual journey and not waste time attempting to educate or change the mind of someone who isn't ready for the information you have to give them.

I'll explain these phases of Human Spiritual Learning in Four Phases, just like the phases of learning previously. Just like we have four grades in the US in each level of schooling we go through, we have four levels of learning within the spiritual school that is this life.

Phase One, Grade One or Level One, however you prefer to refer to these, is the stage of Learning the Rules of being Human. These are the Souls new to being Human and are here getting a feel for and experience of being Human to start to learn the "Rules" of being Human. They learn how it feels to be in a body and live as a spirit inhabiting a human form.

Phase One: Humans tend to be your "Salt of the Earth" type people just existing and going with the flow. Many of them are born, live and die on the same land, in the same town doing the same business as their family has done for generations. They have little to no ambitions for anything more or greater than what they know. They are just here to be in a body and get a feel for this Human incarnation experience.

The flip side to the Phase One level souls can be the sociopaths and psychopaths who don't seem to see or believe in any "Normal" Human rules. They go about oblivious to the natural order of things that most Humans just intuitively and innately know. As abhorrent as this may be to the rest of us, it is just another level of learning on the spiritual path of Humanity. Many of us have had lives in this level and if we had not wouldn't have our natural awareness of "The Rules" as it were.

Phase Two: Humans tend to be our fundamentalist people. Those humans that follow a religious or philosophical doctrine to the letter and cannot see anything outside their particular set of rules for life. They are entrenched into their dogma and will fight to the death to defend their ideologies, because they associate so personally and strongly to that set of rules.

These are the people who have a hard time thinking for themselves beyond their individual doctrine. They cannot see or accept any other way of being and have been known to kill millions in the quest to indoctrinate all others to their way of thinking.

We may not all agree with this level of thinking or their methods of operation, but it is just another level or class on the path of Human Spiritual Growth.

Phase Three: People have gone through the first two phases but haven't quite gotten away from the philosophy of there being a certain set of rules everyone should follow. Phase three people tend to fall into our liberal, vegetarian, left-wing population of environmentalists and PETA protestors.

They do not believe in the "Old Rules" of religions but believe in a new set of rules to "Save the Planet" and are just as fanatical about their set of rules as all of the Fundamentalist Religious folks are. They will tie themselves to a tree, throw paint on fur coat wearers, block traffic in protest of car emissions and big oil, and invent all the fake meat substitutes to try to save the animals.

These people are just the next step up the ladder of evolution. They do not believe in the old rules but still have a set of rules they follow. Their "New Rules" are promoted and followed just as fanatically as Phase Two people follow their set of rules.

These two groups tend to clash a lot in their differing set of rules, trying to prove whose sets of rules are more right and more important. We humans spend a lot of time and lifetimes fighting over an arbitrary set of rules and philosophies for life. And, it is the next phase of people who tend to sit back and shake their heads at all this fighting and misery over a made-up set of "Rules."

Phase Four: People are mostly people like you and me. We've been through the other three phases and have followed all the rules and now we are at a point in our spiritual human development that we understand that there aren't really any hard and fast rules for being a Human. We've gotten past the point of doctrine and dogma to a place of a more open-minded spiritual belief system.

Phase Four people tend to allow others to follow their preferred set of rules without much complaint or issue. They will attempt to plant seeds and influence the other phases away from their dogmatic belief systems, but they don't try too hard to convert any of the more fundamentalist minded humans.

They prefer to stand back and not get caught up in all the drama of belief promotion or defending. It just isn't worth the effort or energy for them. They follow a philosophy of "live and let live" that comes from having lives fighting and defending the varied belief systems in their past lives.

Phase four people are the spiritual, metaphysical, witchy, law of attraction and manifestation people. They are looking past the finite physical experience to a larger spiritual experience outside the limited parameters of a human physical lifespan and 3D sensory experience.

There are also those in transition between phases who still have a foundation in a religious or philosophical set of rules, but who don't hold too tightly to those beliefs and don't demean other people for not sharing their particular beliefs. These transitory people are moving out of one phase into another and in so doing are releasing their need for a certain set of rules to open up to the possibility of their own unique creation as a Human.

For me and most of those I know or have met in either the transition phase or already in phase four, the only rules they follow can be summed up simply as: Do You, Leave Others Alone and Don't Be a Dick.

I think those are easy rules to follow and will save you a lot of stress and drama if you follow them. The choice, of course, is yours.

Chapter Five

A HISTORY OF SEPARATION

Now that we have covered the Big Bang Theory with respect to our nature of Oneness, the phases of learning and spiritual growth we can begin to get into the effects of separating from Oneness into multiple dimensional realities. The upside is we can actually experience things and see, feel, and hear, and aren't confined to the one-dimensional all-in-one paradigm. However, the downside is that with the multiple-dimensional realities that we use for reference, we have an experience of separation and difference from one another.

Since we all have our own groovy little space suit bodies to utilize as an experience vessel from when we jump into it until we decide to jump out of it, we have the illusion of separation between us. This is a wonderful experiential tool because it gives each of us our own unique view and perspective to learn and grow from. No matter what takes place in our lives, our perspective and experience are unique only to each of us individually.

Even twins who share DNA and most everything else are uniquely different people. No matter how alike they are, they still experience their own unique world in their own unique way.

This seeming separation for the purpose of individual experience has led many of us to forget our nature of oneness, especially while in the body. Once out of the body, we are still a unique and individual consciousness, but we are aware of our nature of oneness with all that is, without the constraints of a body. Without the body, we can move at the speed of thought, be in all places at once, and communicate through direct sharing of experience, much like telepathy.

In our physical bodies, we get to experience our own unique personal oneness through our own unique perspective. And, just to spice it up even more, so that we may bring out all the juicy experiences we can from this physical life, our personal perspective is constantly changing, so even if we did have what looks like the same experience again, we wouldn't experience it in the same way as before. Each new moment in our perception of time is a new experience. Each new word I write here on my laptop is a new experience, a brand-new perspective of the same word due to the placement, context, and structure.

Change being the only constant in the universe is a function of design, and if you have the eyes to see and the ears to hear, you will know that this is true. No moment is ever the same. No experience, no matter how seemingly alike, is the same. We are perpetual beings of fluidity, change, and choice. We chose to move from oneness to multiple dimensions of reality to give substance and variety to our experiences. We've chosen these bodies, lives, places, families, and everything else for the sheer purpose of experience itself.

There is nothing like experience. How can you describe love without the experience of it? How can you describe the taste of an orange to someone who has never tasted one? You can try, but the only way to really know a thing is through the experience of it. So, we've designed these lives for the specific and strict purpose of experience.

Yes, we may have some plan or another of the things we would like to accomplish and roles to fulfill in each incarnation of life, but the simple, bare bones reason for it all is "Experience." Period!

This is why we have developed this perception of separation, so that we have all of our personal experiences in our own unique ways, and this adds to the total sum of consciousness to which we all belong. So, the IS that we all come from is added to, grown, and enhanced by every single experience we each have.

There is a history of separation for the purposes of power consolidation, manipulation, and simple greed that has encompassed our planet these last 5,000 years. This, of course, is not in and of itself a bad thing because it is leading us into the golden age of oneness and prosperity that we have all been longing for throughout the last thousand lifetimes or so. We don't do anything without a purpose behind it, and all things fall within the cycles of growth and death, expansion and contraction, and so on. Hopefully, that took a little of the sting out of this next part. It is nice to know that even the seemingly bad things are good when viewed from the viewpoint of wholeness and cycles.

Starting some 5,000 years ago, we started the move into a new cycle of a male-dominated, patriarchal, and capitalistic society of fear, separation from nature, each other, and our sense of oneness. Since the onset of the beginnings of the capitalistic societal model, where the land and cattle began to be hoarded, and people started to believe in scarcity over abundance, a natural trend towards separation has occurred. Since we believed that the only way to have more was to compete with others and that there was only so much to go around, we developed an "us against them" mentality, which separated us further.

As those in power began to gain more and more, their desire and greed also grew, and they began to implement strategies to instill a belief in scarcity, separation, and competition. Simply because the easiest way to get one over on others is to have them fight or compete among themselves, which frees you up to spend your time hoarding it all. By keeping people in fear through a belief in separation, lack, and competition, the class structures were formed, and the haves began to control and manipulate the have-nots. This is pretty much the state of the world we live in today. The elitist few control the majority of the so-called power on the planet.

Yet, I would like to take this opportunity to point out that the "power" they have is nothing more than an illusion of power. The money they control most of us with is an illusion. It is not real; it has no substance and is based on nothing more than a perpetuated belief in its necessity and the control of it. Our country was founded by those wishing to free themselves from the central banking system of England and to form a free-market society based on trade and not control. Yet, the central banking families waited patiently and bided their time until 1913, when the Federal Reserve Act was signed in secret on Jekyll Island by the ruling families of the time. And, since then we have been in one war after another and one recession, depression or inflationary period after another. All meticulously designed and perpetrated by those in control, to consolidate the assets and wealth of the world for them.

The plan, plain and simple, is for world domination and control. Why, you ask. Because addiction is addiction, and when you have everything you ever wanted, the only thing you could want would be more, or everything. These families are all addicted to control and power and the accumulation of it. They care nothing for sustainability, practicality, community, peace, or harmony. They can't help themselves. Like any other addict, jonesing for their fix, these few elitist families have a compulsion to accumulate, acquire, and control everything they see. Honestly, they really can't help themselves. They are slaves to their addiction. Their Addiction, or DEVIL, if you will, is accumulation and control.

The silver lining to this whole scenario is simply this: All the work they have been doing for the last several hundred years to monopolize and own the world will work to the benefit of all people on this planet. As they gather up companies, corporations, countries, and resources and in so doing erase borders and currencies and governments in hopes of controlling everything, they are breaking down all the barriers for us to become one united global community with one currency and governing body.

This unification will allow the free flow of commerce and trade in the near future which will abolish poverty and scarcity on the planet. In addition, there will be the inception of many new free energy and renewable energy technologies, which have been kept away from the general public by those same few. These families have put in all this work building a global infrastructure to try to rule us, and we will gratefully and graciously take the keys from them and utilize that infrastructure to bring about the new Golden Age for all of humanity.

All of that was to illustrate the main reasons behind the designed influence of limiting and separatist belief systems by the socio-economic systems of today. The negative and fear-based news broadcasts are designed to keep us in fear of others and, in so doing, in fear of ourselves.

When all you see is danger on every corner and in every street, you are living out of fear and out of your natural power. Which makes us all far easier to control, because we have been broken and tamed by fear and separation.

Nowadays, all you see is "us against them" all over the news and "you are not good enough the way you are" images and articles in every magazine and advertisement on television, radio, and internet sites. We are inundated with reasons to dislike, doubt, and downright hate our own reflections in the mirror.

All that separatist thinking is, in many ways, a natural aftereffect of the Big Bang explosion into the multi-dimensional realities we find ourselves in today. With each new dimension giving us more and more reference points to use, we find it easier and easier to nit-pick every little detail of people and our lives in the world today. So much so, that we have lost sight of almost everything else and can only focus on the differences. All we see are how others are different from us, and usually in a very judgmental fear-based way. All we notice are differences like race, color, sexual preference and nationality, or style of dress, taste in music, choice of car, home, and job. Thankfully, the cyclical nature of the universe has already provided us with the answer and paved the way for our golden future.

As with every tidal ebb and flow, so do our lives, nations, and world follow the same cyclical framework. All so-called evil in this world that we have experienced and recorded in our histories is a prelude to goodness and expansion. The greatest and most awful of tragedies inspires the greatest and most loving responses from us.

In many ways, the "Facing the Devil in You" concept is an acknowledgment of the force of, and necessity of, cycles in our lives. Every so-called evil or trauma that transpired in our lives can lead to the greatest good and wisdom, if acknowledged, accepted, understood, and utilized. More good comes from acknowledging pain and failure than from blessings and gifts. The Creator or God teaches us best through what we would consider Devilish means.

This current cycle can be described as a contractive cycle in which we are realizing the illusion of separation and the truth of our divine oneness. We have explored every degree imaginable of our belief in separation, fear, and lack. Now we are coming to the logical next conclusion of unity, wholeness, and abundance.

Old tribal traditions and teachings are returning to the forefront of our conscious experience to remind us of our connection to all things and our interconnected nature. So, in effect, we are contracting from a consciousness of separation and difference back to one of wholeness, oneness, and similarity or sameness. This process is speeding up as we all become more aware of and in tune with our inner nature and more natural state of being.

There has been an ever-increasing influx of energy from the galactic center onto our planet starting around 1987 with the cosmic convergence, taking us through 2012 and out into the future. Many tribal traditions believe we are heading into an age of a thousand years of light. And, judging from our position in the cosmos and our entering into the photon band, which we will be fully immersed in for the next two thousand years, I'd say that is highly possible, if not probable.

All the focus on differences between us has basically run its course, and now there is a natural inclination to forget the differences and focus on the similarities. Coincidence, I'd like to think not, but you can be your own judge.

Unfortunately, like with most periods of change, it is a double-edged sword. For all the progress in the direction of unity and oneness, there is also a digging in of the heels, so to speak, and a holding onto those limited belief systems by those who fear change and progress. There is a push within the media and government agencies to highlight these differences in a fear-mongering campaign to keep us separated and in fear of anyone different from us in any way.

Yet even that approach is failing. Just recently, there was a push towards a war between Israel and Iran by their governments and media. An online movement by the people to stop the proposed war and bombing created a worldwide buzz and the message of this movement was "I don't hate you. I don't even know you. How could I hate someone I don't even know?"

How powerful and moving is that? It's as amazing as it is telling. We are creating our own change and riding this wave of new higher vibrational energy right into the new Golden Age. It is all a matter of focus. What are you focused on, the negative media and propaganda or the positive movement of the people towards love and acceptance?

Where your attention goes, your energy flows. Keep that in mind while you go throughout your day. Nothing says you must watch the news and be inundated by all that separatist propaganda. You could go for a walk in nature and smile at the people you pass by. That little shift in your day will have a ripple effect across the entire world.

We are naturally beginning to lean back into connection and oneness with our fellow humans and like with most change, the first step is to change our minds about ourselves. We are not lone individuals lost in the desert fighting to survive, as most mainstream ideology professes. We are connected to everyone and everything. No matter how hard we try to pretend we are alone in the world, it just isn't true. In our most isolated and cut off physical state, we still are connected to God, the universe, your guides, spirit family and so much more.

Once you begin to accept that you are not alone, you begin to see the evidence of this, and you see how you are connected to everyone and everything. The only reason it seemed like you felt like you were alone was because you created the belief that you were a separate being from the whole and our loving universe gives you the experience of what you believe to be true. This is why I am constantly saying, "Believing is Seeing." Your beliefs create your experience of reality.

The best part of the realization and taking responsibility for your creation of your experience of reality, is you have the power to change it as you see fit. Just have patience when you start to change your mind and your reality. It took you this long to get to where you are now. It won't take as long to change your mind to something you prefer to create, but it won't happen overnight either.

Our physical neuropathways in our brains take time to change from one belief and habit to another. The common belief is that it takes 28 days to change a habit. And that's just one habit. It will take you some time to change all your beliefs and habits. Have patience with yourself and give yourself grace in the process.

Luckily for all of us in this very process of Facing the Devil in You, metaphysics is now teaching us that our multi-dimensional nature means that whatever it is we wish to create in our lives already exists in a parallel reality and the fastest way to experience that change is to align with the version of ourselves that already has what we want.

Who would you be if you had all that you desired? How would you act? How would you feel? What would you do when you woke up in the morning having every-thing you could want?

Begin to think, feel and model that version of yourself in the present moment and watch your reality shift in miraculous ways. Continue to remind yourself that your present reality is just a mirror of your past beliefs and thoughts. As you shift and live as if you already had all you wanted, stay consistent and do not use your current situation to deter you from what you are manifesting and creating in your life.

Just as in The Matrix, Neo had to first believe, not know, but believe from "Balls to Bones" as the Oracle put it, that he was The One before he became The One and did the miracles he did. The same is true for us as well. We must practice our new reality, knowing that we already have it in another dimension, until we believe it so fully that our reality has no choice but to become that which we believe.

Understanding that you are not only not separate but truly connected to all that is and to all versions of you in the unlimited potential of the universe will help you on your way to creating that which you truly desire.

The only catch to this is what you contracted to experience as a spirit before coming into the body. Almost everyone I've ever met, prior to their awakening to their true spiritual nature, has said that they would not have chosen the craziness they experienced in life. However, they forget their true spiritual eternal nature and the desire of that side of them to experience all potentials and possibilities on the Earth plane to learn all that they can from all possible experiences.

This awareness begins to help us see that we are not a victim to some Evil Outside Devil here to trick us into selling our souls, but that we have just forgotten that we chose and why we chose to experience this particular set of life circumstances. Everything that we experience The Source also experiences and as we grow in learning and experiences, so too does The Source.

This illusion of separation that we are living in is part of the grand plan of growth, experience, and wisdom set up by our source creator to learn and grow as much as IT can. We are not victims but willing participants in the on-going expansion of the Universe as a whole.

You are in partnership with everyone and everything around you to create as many potential realities as possible. You are connected to all that exists and have the power to create as you see fit. As long as what you wish to create aligns with your personal Soul Mission here on the Earth Plane.

Often this is the hardest pill to swallow on your personal spiritual awakening journey. The Red Pill of responsibility for everything that happens in your life.

You are the creator and co-creator of everything you see and experience around you. This acknowledgment and awareness is the first step towards your personal power and freedom. You must accept responsibility for everything in your life. Once you do, you are free to create or re-create whatever you want.

You are not separate from anything but merely playing a little game of hide-and-seek with your greater self for a while so that you can have a unique experience of creation. Once you know this, Balls to Bones, as it were, you'll take your power back and start the magical journey as your own personal alchemist in your story of creation.

Chapter Six

THE DISEASE OF DUALITY

To begin this chapter, I would like to explain the chapter title a little to get you thinking along the same lines as I am so that the rest of the book will hopefully make more sense. I realize that the title may seem a bit overboard for a book like this, but if we break it down a little, I think you'll agree with me that it is very appropriate.

Let's start with "Disease." Disease or Dis-ease is a state in which you or your body is out of balance in some way causing a myriad of symptoms, issues, and if not corrected, death. I'm sure we are all very aware of what we commonly consider disease and sickness, but this out-of-balance nature can also be found in many other areas of life as well. Our thinking is an area that is rife with dis-ease.

We believe that we are separated from every other being on the planet and thereby different. We are taught that the world is rife with evil and that our purpose in life is to prove ourselves worthy of the blessings of an almighty being who is separate from us and out there somewhere in the universe passing judgment on all of mankind like a child with an ant farm and a magnifying glass. With this ingrained belief about the world we live in it is no wonder that we as a race and a species are overrun with disease and sickness.

We are taught and taught over and over again that the big bad world out there is out to get us and that we have to do whatever it takes to survive. Apparently, those in charge of our curriculum believe that it is better to teach separation and lack than wholeness and abundance. Of course, this is the case, not out of sheer spite, in most cases, but out of a true belief that we are all separate entities on this planet who don't belong to the whole of the biosphere and must fight, steal and cheat to "win."

Thankfully most of those old ways of thinking are being shifted from the belief in separation and the survival of the fittest to a more inclusive and cooperative mindset. Yet this is not without its inherent difficulties. Our whole system is based on theories that have little to no basis in actuality and truth. Yet, they have been taught and practiced for so long that the majority of the people believe those beliefs are the truth and all that is. Therefore, it is up to people like you and I to gently show those still in the old belief paradigm the truth and beauty of wholeness.

As an example of an old theory whose time has come to be replaced, let us review Darwin's Theories of Evolution and Survival of the Fittest. If you have had the privilege to hear some of our new thought teachers such as Gregg Braden speak of his research into Darwin's Theories and studies then you probably know where I am going with this, but in case you haven't, then I will summarize for you and if you want more information on this subject, I encourage you to delve deeper and do some research of your on as well.

Basically, when Darwin wrote his book on Evolution, he left room for his theories to be expanded upon and even outright dismissed. In his own hand he wrote that if any of his findings were found to be false, then the whole of his research would very probably then be false. Since Darwin did his main research on the Galápagos Islands, an isolated ecosystem almost devoid of any outside influence, his research at the outset was flawed. He made wide sweeping assumptions about nature based on a very small, isolated example of the whole.

For example, Darwin observed an anthill on one section of the island and noticed that the ants tended to be aggressive and fight among themselves for food and domination. Then he theorized that if these ants did this, then the whole of the animal kingdom was in competition for food and lived in a fight for survival. Based on these observations the whole basis for science was born. The majority of our scientific theory is based solely on the false assumptions of a man who in his own hand wrote that if any part of his research was wrong, then the whole of his research was faulty. Darwin knew that there was likely, if not assuredly, a different version of events unfolding within the animal kingdom and all of nature. Yet, this is still the accepted scientific theory which is taught throughout schools to this day.

All one has to do is turn on the Discovery Channel or History Channel to see proof that Darwin's theories are mistaken and therefore wrong at their very core. The animal community and nature are symbiotic organisms based on cooperation and cohabitation. Wolves, lions, dolphins, dogs hunt in packs. Bees, ants, termites and much of the insect world work together for the good of the whole. When predators kill, they usually go for the weak and sick and only eat what they need. There is no greed within the animal community. There is no hoarding of food or resources, unless you want to claim that squirrels storing up nuts for the winter is hoarding instead of good planning.

Now, this is a very basic example of an intricate and much deeper subject. There are those who are far better qualified to expand on these theories than I am, but I hope that this will spark an interest within you to go do more research and find out more for yourself. So that you may spread the word and become a part of the change in this world from competition to wholeness and cooperation.

We are all a part of a symbiotic unit that has long ago failed and needs to be recuperated for the future survival of all of us. Luckily for us, there are those who are already aware of this growing need and are taking steps towards the future. People like Jacque Fresco and his Venus Project, which is a model of a resourced based economy, are potentially an answer to our current crisis. Those people who are learning to live off the grid in sustainable conscious living communities who utilize solar, wind and geothermal energy are examples of our potential future.

We are not the apex predator or the peak of evolution and therefore free to do whatever we please in our race of greed and expansion toward our inevitable doom. We are a part of a living, connected, and symbiotic organism that has been around for billions of years and will be around for billions more. The question is, will we be?

This Disease of Duality has infiltrated and influenced every part of our human society and has been the reason for all wars in the past 5,000 years of our existence. We believe that we can own things and therefore must protect what we own from others. We believe that the ideas in our heads are who we are and therefore we must protect those as well from others who disagree with us. We have believed that when we arrive in an area that is new to us that we have the right and privilege to just take what we want with no regard for those that are already there or who came before us. We actually believe that because we come in two different gender bodies that one must be superior to the other due to what, physical strength?

All of these notions are preposterous, and any open-minded aware person will tell you as much. But we are still dealing with the repercussions and ramifications of all these flawed belief systems in the world today. Yet, there is hope on the horizon. We are being stirred at our core by energies from the core of the universe. We are being shifted and awakened to our true nature. We have all felt this stirring deep within our souls to awaken and expand. We have been triggered and are responding in kind.

The tribal wisdoms are being rediscovered. Ancient stories are being told again. The ceremonies for peace and wholeness with Mother Earth have been growing in frequency and power over the last twenty years. There is hope for us and a bright future ahead of us. All that is required of us is simply this: Let go of your old beliefs and open your heart to the truth of your being. You are one with source and all that is. You are a part of God, The Universe, The Source, of All. Remember your place in the cosmos and your calling as a unique divine representation of the One.

The beauty of this elixir for the Disease of Duality is in its simplicity. Just let go of your old, outdated belief systems and feel into your heart where the truth of your connection to everything lies. It is so simple that most of you will dismiss, deny and denounce this for a long time to come. But the truth will shine through, and when the time comes, you will have but one choice. You will either choose the old ways of fear or you will choose Love. It is that simple.

You are not who you have been taught you are. You are not a number. You are not a nationality. You are not a Race. You are not an income or credit score. You are not a man or a woman. You are not even what you think of yourself. You ARE pure source energy expressing itself in the physical for a short time to create and expand the universe. You are God in the flesh, perfect and whole and exactly who, what and where you need to be. As hard as all this may be for you to accept at this point in your life, try to remember this; The Universe doesn't make mistakes. Everything is in perfect harmony with the system and is as special and necessary as any other part. You are exactly what God needs you to be. Follow your heart, follow your dreams and be exactly who you are meant to be, YOU. That is all that you have to do. Do what inspires you and makes you happy and you will be fulfilling your God-given purpose.

You are no longer a separate entity who is lost in a world that doesn't love you. You are a special and unique piece of divinity put here to fulfill your special calling, to be exactly who you are and to play your part in this great symbiotic machine called life, the planet, the universe,… God.

Those of you who are in a female body at the moment, you are not separate from those in a male body. Those of you in a male body, you are not separate from those in a female body. And, for those of you who don't believe me… try to survive without the other. No matter what form you are in now, you have been in the other before. No matter what function you are fulfilling now, you have fulfilled the other previously. No matter who you think you are, you are that and yet *SO MUCH MORE!*

We are not simply male or female, black or white, American or Arab; we are people, we are source, we are God made manifest in the flesh, and we are all perfectly designed to fulfill our special function here on Earth.

And now that you have read these words and felt this message within your heart and soul,… I'm sorry, but you can never go back. You know too much now, and you are no longer capable of accepting anything less than your true divinity. I'm sure many of you will try. Hell, I know I have! Over and over again, but the truth remains, and I have to accept it just as you will have to accept it. You are divine, you are perfect, you are eternal, and you are you and so much more.

The Disease of Duality is a disease of the mind. The cure is love and acceptance of yourself and your truest nature. Love is who you are. Love is what you are made of. You cannot deny that which you are anymore. You can live without love as well as you can live without air, or water or food. Love is essential to your nature and your soul. Love is what we are all made of and cannot be denied or replaced. We can lie to ourselves for a while and many of us still are. But, in the end, there is only Love, and that is all there is.

In the context of this book, we will need to acknowledge that if Love is all there is, then Love is a Spectrum. Just like we have a spectrum of light, sound, magnetism, and the like, love is also a spectrum. That spectrum ranges from the unlimited Love of Source that we all originated from, to the depths of fear and separation that we get to experience here on the Earth Plane.

Facing the Devil in You and your life is much more easily accomplished when you realize that the Devil is just one end of the Spectrum of Love. It is the personification of the absence or lack of love. The separation and fear we experience in life is just us being on the opposite end of the spectrum than we started from. Just as in every day we can swing from unconditional love to outright hatred and fear, so too can we swing back into unconditional love and acceptance.

Your journey with your own personal Devil is your own journey and exploration of the Spectrum of Love from one end to the other and back again. The Devil is not separate from God, but just the other end of the spectrum of God. Just as there is no "Dark Switch" on the wall, only an absence of light when the light switch is turned off. There is no being different from God, called the Devil, but just our own personification of our own darkness as we swing away from the light of love.

You yourself is a spectrum of all capacities and capabilities from love to fear and hatred. You have the ability and right to chose any part of this vast spectrum for your exploration and learning. We all come to the Earth Plane to experience the illusion of separation, fear and evil. These are our greatest teachers on this plane and invariably will lead us back to the Love and Light of God as we continue our lifetimes of exploration into the depths of darkness.

Darkness and fear are our greatest teachers of love and light. We cannot know light within the light; we can only experience true light from the absence of it. You are not forsaken from God, but merely taking a step back to get a fuller perspective of what God is.

There is a favorite parable of mine that illustrates this point.

THE LITTLE FLAME AND THE SUN

Once upon a time there was a little flame who lived as part of the great Sun of the Universe. And this little flame was so in love with and in awe of the great Sun that one day the little Flame said to the great Sun:

The Little Flame said:

"Oh, Great Sun, how can I know you better? How can I be like you and know my light?"

The Great Sun replied:

"Do you truly want to know your own light as I do?

The Little Flame replied:

"Oh yes! I want that very much!"

The Great Sun:

"Are you sure that you want to truly know your own light as I do? Will you do whatever it takes to know your light?"

The Little Flame:

"Oh yes, I will do anything to know my light!"

The Great Sun said:

"Then you will need to know darkness."

The Little Flame asks:

"What is Darkness?"

The Great Sun:

"Darkness is the absence of light. The absence of me. Are you prepared to know darkness?"

The Little Flame, a little less sure of itself now says: "Ohh.. I'm not sure I understand. What do you mean darkness is the absence of light, the absence of you?"

The Great Sun replies:

"You see, all you have known is the light that is me. You were born within me and have known nothing but the light and warmth that is me. Therefore, you cannot truly know light, when that is all you've ever experienced. To truly know light and your own light you must go from me and experience darkness and cold."

In surprise the Little Flame says:

"I must go from you to know my light truly? I'm not sure I understand what that means, but I am willing to do whatever it takes to know my light."

With a great sigh, the Great Sun said:

"If you are sure, you truly want to know your light, then I will send you into darkness."

And with a wave of his great Sun hand, the Great Sun sent the Little Flame out into the darkness and void of space all by itself.

As you can imagine, this was a great shock to the Little Flame, who had only ever known the light and warmth of the great sun. Now, floating in the darkness and quiet of space all by itself, the little flame began to shiver and cry.

Little Flame:

"Oh no! Oh, Great Sun, why have you forsaken me?! Why have you sent me away from you? What did I do to deserve this banishment?! Did I not worship you enough? How did I wrong you?!"

In its great knowing and wisdom, the Great Sun did not answer the Little Flame's pleas and cries. He left the Little Flame alone to work it out and learn for itself.

After some time went by the Little Flame began to notice there was light in the darkness. It became accustomed to the darkness and started to see its own light shining in the darkness.

It was small and dim, but its light shone brighter in the darkness and illuminated the space around the little flame so that it could see and feel its own warmth.

This revelation was a shock to the Little Flame, but it gave the Little Flame great joy to see its own light shining and to feel its own warmth from its light.

As the Little Flame became aware of its own light and warmth, that light gave it great joy and with that great joy the Little Flame began to grow into a bigger, brighter and warmer light in the darkness. As the Little Flame grew and grew, it began to know its own light and warmth. Surrounded by darkness and quiet and coldness, the Little Flame shone brighter and brighter and knew its own light.

As the Little Flame began to grow brighter and brighter, the Great Sun smiled down upon the Little Flame and said:

"I see you, Little Flame, shining bright in the darkness. I see you now know your own light. Are you ready to come back to me and be a part of the Great Sun again?"

With a smile of great pride, the Little Flame said:

"Oh Great Sun, thank you, thank you, thank you! I appreciate your offer and will come back to you some day, but for now, I would like to explore my own light and shine it bright for the rest to see in the darkness."

And so, with a loving smile on both the face of the Great Sun and the Little Flame, they both went on shining in the darkness and quiet for all the rest of creation to see.

Ohh. Don't you just love that story? I know I do.

It illustrates very simply how we all are sent away from the Source to learn about and to know our own light in the darkness. How to be the little light from the great sun in the darkness, shining bright and warm for all to see.

This is you and me. We are all the Little Flames, out in the darkness, representing the Great Sun of creation as only we can, in our own unique expression of the great Source of all that is.

Please keep on shining your light for the world, and if you aren't feeling bright enough, maybe me helping you to Face the Devil in You will give you the power to brighten your light in the world and to shine like the piece of the Great Sun that you truly are.

Chapter Seven

THE FUNCTION OF THE EGO

The Ego is one of those enigmatic things that we have a hard time pinning down in a simple description. I have spent many hours, days, and weeks, it seems, going over this subject within myself and with others. I have read countless pages about the Ego and its perceived function.

In many teachings, the EGO could be replaced with the term "DEVIL" very easily. So many teachings tell us we need to control, suppress, or kill the Ego for self-mastery. And yet, that seems a far too simplistic and dualistic-minded concept of the Ego. All that we are is a reflection of the Creator, and if we are perfect as the Creator made us, why would we need to "KILL" a part of ourselves for self-mastery? Isn't it more likely that we just haven't understood or utilized the Ego properly?

Sitting in my Course in Miracles class one Tuesday evening, when one of the other participants asked our teacher, "What does the Course say the function of the Ego is?" As she gave her explanation from her perspective of the Course in Miracles, I sat on pins and needles because spirit had just downloaded a thought into my head, and it was all I could do to keep my seat and my composure at that moment. When there was an appropriate opening, I raised my hand and said with all due certainty, "The Ego is a contrast detection device. Its function is to show us contrast so that we may have more information and make better choices."

The EGO, in and of itself, is neither good nor bad. It is just a program running in our Mind-Body-Spirit Matrix that is solely focused on our physical survival. Which is why it can be such a troublesome and worrisome part of us. When any of us become too focused on one thing above all others, we become out of balance, and if allowed to go on long enough, we become diseased and eventually die due to the chronic imbalance.

With the EGO's singular focus on our physical bodies' survival, it can adopt some altogether unhealthy habits in an attempt to ensure homeostasis. Our EGOs would rather us stay stuck and the same, rather than challenge our personal status quo in an attempt to better things.

This is why it can be so hard to change habits, even when we truly want to because we know that habit is bad for us. The EGO wants things to stay the same. As far as the EGO is concerned, the same is safe and controllable.

So, as the infinite divine operators of this physical human suit, it is up to us to override and convince the EGO that we know better and that it will be far happier with the upgrades we are planning to implement.

You see, from the EGO's perspective an addiction to a substance is a good thing. Because, that substance that we abuse, makes our bodies "Feel Better," at least for a time. The EGO's physically focused attention is all about keeping the body alive in the short term. Obtaining homeostasis today, no matter the consequences tomorrow.

Just like a child addicted to sweets, the EGO will crave, cry, scream and throw fits for that sweet, no matter how bad we may know it is for us, the EGO does not care, it wants its sweets.

What is needed to retrain the EGO, in the same way we would train a dog or a child, is positive reinforcement of the things we want to reframe and retrain in our lives. The EGO only knows what it knows and like any other part of us, change seems terrifying to the EGO. It is the "Great Unknown" out there that the EGO fears. All things NEW are UNKNOWN and therefore, in the EGO's opinion, dangerous and to be avoided at all costs.

Utilizing patience and positive reinforcement we can retrain any part of ourselves, even the ever-stubborn EGO, to comply with the changes we wish to implement. It's just a matter of clearly defining the end goal and using those positive reinforcement treats and tricks to keep our little EGOs compliant and onboard with the changes we wish to make.

Just as we have to do when working with children and pets, remember that logic is a "four-letter" word to them. Feeling and emotion are the driving forces for the EGO. So, using positive reinforcement and little rewards we can integrate and retrain the EGO to be our best buddy in the process of change and growth.

Let me reiterate, if I haven't beaten this particular horse to death yet. Your EGO is not BAD. Your EGO does not need to be KILLED. Your EGO only needs love and understanding. Your EGO needs you to listen to its motives and drives, so that you'll understand that everything it does, no matter how seemingly negative it is, is done with love in mind and a wish for your very survival to continue.

Your EGO loves you and wants you to Live!!

Stop trying to KILL the EGO and learn to LOVE it as you would any other misbehaving child or pet. Your EGO is crying out for love and understanding, just like you are. Give it love and understanding and you'll create your best and most potent ally in life.

One way to help you love and accept your Ego, is to continue with your Shadow and Inner Child work. The deeper you go down your own personal Rabbit Hole of personality and being, the more you will understand what your egoic forces within you are attempting to do.

Every part of you, within you, is working towards the same goal of keeping you safe and alive, in their own unique ways. Which, understandably, is a bit of a mess to deal with. All these different parts of you with their own priorities fighting to keep you safe and alive in the best way that they see fit.

I mean, imagine this as an example. Go to your next family reunion, stand up on the table in the middle of dinner and yell out to your whole family that you have a problem and that you need help with said problem... How do you imagine that little scenario will play out for you?

I would imagine that it would be fodder for nightmare fuel. Every different family member that you have, telling you what you need to do to fix your issue. I mean, what could possibly go wrong?

Now that you've shaken off the shiver that just ran down your spine, let's dive into the differing parts of your Ego. And to answer the question that may have just popped into your mind. No, you don't have just one Ego. Your Ego is made up of parts, just like you are. Just like your body is. Just like your mind is. Your Ego is made up of parts and all those parts want to keep you safe and in turn, keep them safe and alive as well.

The parts of your Ego are made up of the same parts of your mind that are covered in Internal Family Therapy, which we will deal with in later chapters. For now, let us just say that every little child part of you that broke off due to trauma and incidents that your little child self didn't have the tools to deal with, became the parts of your Ego that are now fighting among themselves to keep you safe and alive in its own way.

Many of the voices that are arguing within you with every decision you try to make are those same parts of you that want to keep you small and safe from harm. Those self-sabotaging parts of you that scream for you to play small and insignificant so that you don't draw attention, because attention is dangerous. Attention will bring judgment and ridicule and spiteful anger from all those who do not wish the best for you. And it will also bring judgment and advice from all those who love you or, at least, say that they love you, because they want to keep you safe as well and in the same form that they are used to you being in.

Each of your loved ones' Egos will try to downplay you and keep you where they like you, where they can control you, and where they can understand you to keep them safe and sound in their little bubbles of experience. They do not mean to do it. They want to be supportive and encouraging, but they just can't because it goes against all their Egoic programming to keep the status quo, because the status quo equals safety.

However, it is very hard for our Egos and the Egos of our loved ones to see past their own blinders of trauma, fear of change and anxiety around being left behind or replaced, as you grow and mature along your own life path. Some of the greatest critics and anchors to our forward movement in life are our own egos and those of our loved ones who "want the best" for us, but can't help themselves from holding us back.

Like the crabs in the bucket who will pull back any crab that tries to climb out, so to do our own egos and those of our families keep us held back. Not out of malice, but out of love for us and a desire to keep us safe.

I remember, in my own experience, my father was highly critical and demeaning of my dreams, not because he didn't want me to achieve them, but because he didn't want me to feel the sting of disappointment. He was trying to save me from failure and disappointment by being so critical and demeaning that I didn't want to even try for my dreams any longer.

He loved me, but like many other loved ones, his love was directed by his unconscious Ego, which was full of fear for me and for himself. What if I did achieve my dreams and exceed his achievements? What would that mean about him? What would that mean for our relational dynamics? What would that mean about the future for us?

So often we are kept safe and small by those that love us most and by ourselves due to the fear of change and the fear of the unknown. Our own Egos will keep us safe and small, stuck in familiar patterns, even if they will ultimately be detrimental, because it is the known and the known is seen as safe. Whether the known is actually safe or not, is of no consequence to our Ego. It is the known, and the known is manageable. The known is not the unknown to be feared. It is what is and we know what is because we've already been there and done that.

This is the childish logic that runs our Egos and most of our minds here. If you've ever wondered why the so-called "Adult World" seems like a bunch of eight-year-olds running around the playground playing hide and seek from each other while trying to manipulate the game in their favor, well now you have a better idea why.

Our Egos are formed in our earliest years and rarely mature out of this childish phase of thinking without much therapy and inner child work by our adult selves. You can reprogram your Egos to actually be beneficial to you and your future dreams, but it will take a lot of inner child work and re-parenting of our inner selves to get your Egos to be on the same page as your dreams.

We all need to re-parent our inner children and show them it is safe to come out and play and that the future unknown isn't as deadly as our childish Egoic minds think it is. We've made it this far and survived, relatively unscathed. We can handle the rest of what life has to offer as well.

Facing the Devil in you is all about re-parenting your inner child parts back into wholeness with your adult self. The Devil we face is the blocked and stagnant energy from that exiled inner child expression that is looking for release and flow.

Chapter Eight

THIS AND THAT

Much of what we as humans today deal with is this notion of This or That. It's either black OR white, Good OR Bad, Right OR Wrong, Man OR Woman, etc..

I believe this mindset or belief system is at the core of much of what ails us as humanity. We are attempting to divide ourselves into one or the other factions based on our childhood, upbringing, moral education or the nation we live in. It seems that there are as many This OR That's or Right OR Wrong, if you will, as there are families, communities, religions, languages and hair colors in this reality.

It is very difficult to live a life of authenticity to one's own inner guidance when all we have been taught is that at least half of who we are is bad, wrong or evil and must therefore be resisted, ignored, punished or fought against. It doesn't make a whole lot of sense that we would be created in the perfect image of the creator of all that is and yet, be half bad, half wrong as a person. How can we amplify our goodness while at the same time ignoring and stuffing our "Badness"?

Which begs the question... What is "Badness"? What is "Wrong"? What is "Evil"? What is the "Devil"?

As with most of these concepts in our human existence, the reality of such things is relative and varying depending on the individual person you are interacting with. Many times, that person's belief system on the subject of good and bad is specifically predicated on where, when, and how they grew up and the effectiveness of those who raised them as their parents or guardians. The thought patterns that color what one considers good, bad or indifferent are so closely tied to their upbringing that such preferences can be nye on indistinguishable from the person themselves.

We believe what we believe because that's what we were taught to believe by our upbringing, circumstances, experiences and individual personality. Two siblings growing up in the same home with the same parents can come out of childhood with very different concepts of their parent, as well as right, wrong, good and bad. However, in either case, each child received their preferences from their childhood experiences. Each just defined those experiences in a different way.

This may be a good time to tackle a concept that will come in very handy as we continue this dialogue.

THE EVENT VS. STORY PARADOX

In every moment of our lives, we are having experiences, and our individual operating systems are decoding each event to create a specific meaning that aligns with our unique view of the world.

Events in and of themselves are neutral. There is NO inherent meaning in any event at all. No matter what the event is… Yes, even that one!

The examples of this are as many and as varied as the humans you pass on the street every day. One person loves sunshine and rainbows and quiet times. The next person loves Black and dark and eardrum splitting music. Another loves to drive fast and race cars. Then there are those so terrified of driving and flying at high speeds that they'd prefer to take the bus or the train and get to their destination in their own sweet and safe time.

To illustrate the point further, your preferences change throughout your life. When you are young, all you want to be is older and grown up. Once you grow up, all you want to be is young again. Your preferences change from one phase of life to the next. For example, I used to love to be out every night drinking and partying. Now I prefer to avoid bars, clubs and any place full of too-loud music and inebriated people.

There is no right or wrong, good or bad event, there is just your preference today. Your preferences will change with your mood. An event that one day thrills and excites you, will disgust and repel you the next day.

Every event is neutral. A thing happens and then we make up what it means to each of us individually. This internal storytelling is the root and cause of much of our own individual misery or triumphs. The Events don't matter. The stories we tell ourselves about those events do.

I do realize that it can be hard to accept the idea of there being no intrinsic right or wrong. Evey time this discussion comes up someone will invariably say; "So murder isn't wrong? Killing people isn't wrong? Rape, stealing, kidnapping, slavery, these things aren't wrong?" And my answer is always, it depends on your perspective.

The higher your perspective, the less wrong things become. You begin to see the divine synchronicity of life and that no one is ever a victim of anyone else. We are all co-creating this thing we call reality and life. No one is a victim of another; we all play our part in this big play called life.

Your thoughts and energy create your experience, so be careful what you believe and think. Where your attention goes, your energy flows. Which is why there is so much mind control and manipulation in the "so-called" news today. If they can keep us scared of some fake imminent catastrophe and mad at "Those People" over there, then we will create and attract those same frequencies into our life experiences.

Just like changing the channel on your TV to a new program, your thoughts and beliefs change and align your frequency to the reality you are most closely a match to. When you change your mind and raise your frequency, so too does your channel or created reality change.

The evidence is found in many of the crime shows and documentaries we've all seen over the years. Criminals are attracted to those on the frequency of a victim. They are not attracted to, nor do they even see those who do not align with the energy of a victim. Watch any documentary or interview with a criminal and you will hear them tell you how they chose their victims and who they avoided.

It's the same with vibes and energy. The reason some people resonate with you and others repel you is all based on frequency and energy. If you would listen to your gut more and trust your instincts more, you would find yourself having far fewer issues with users, abusers, and energy parasites in your life.

Everything is energy, and every energy has a frequency. Energy and Frequencies do not lie. People lie, faces lie, we even lie to ourselves. But energy and frequency do not lie. Trust what you feel about another and don't allow your monkey mind to talk you into something that your gut is telling you to avoid.

I know I have lied to myself and deceived myself about someone else because I wanted something from them or thought I was wrong about what their energy/vibe was telling me about them. Many of us can look back on a failed and traumatic relationship from our past and see how we lied to and deceived ourselves about what we truly felt on our first meeting with that person.

You are an intuitive being and your intuition does not lie to you. If we take the time to listen to our gut feelings and intuition more often, the smoother and more synchronous our lives become. Your intuition is your guide in this life. Just like your GPS in your car or on your phone, it will get you to where you want to go. Maybe not in the way you think is best, but in the way that is best for you. You cannot see the whole journey. You do not know what is around the next corner or bend in the road, but your intuition does. Listen to it. You'll be happy you did.

Your intuition does not judge the rightness or wrongness of a person or situation. It merely guides you towards what is more right for you and towards what you would most prefer. Preference is neither a right or a wrong, it is just a resonance of and matching of frequencies. Your frequency with that of the other person or event. Quiet your mind and listen to your gut and you will be guided toward more matching and synchronous people and events along your journey.

As Bashar, an Interdimensional First Contact Specialist channeled by Daryl Anka, states in his Formula for life:

THE FORMULA HAS THREE PARTS:

1) Act on your highest excitement in every moment.

2) Act on that excitement to the best of your ability.

3) Act on your highest excitement with zero insistence on the outcome or how it should be.

This three-step formula will take time to master, like any new skill, but if followed, practiced and mastered in your own way, you will find your life changing in miraculous ways. The fact that you are focusing your attention and energy on your highest excitement to the best of your ability in every moment means you will create and experience more and more excitement in more and more moments of your life. Your focus creates your reality, and your reality is made up of the experiences of the things you focus on and create.

This is why there is nothing in your experience that is intrinsically bad or wrong, there is just that which you have been focusing on from a lower vibrational frequency and bringing into your experience based on that focus. Change your focus and you will change your life. Focus on that which you prefer and want to experience, and you will crate and attract those things you prefer.

This is not magic or voodoo or any other form of Witchcraft; this is the law of attraction, a universal law.

To quote Bashar again on the 5 Universal Laws or 5 Laws of the Universe, he states:

THE 5 LAWS ARE:

1) You exist. You can't do anything about that. You exist and therefore cannot not exist. That which exist, exists.

2) Everything is here and now. There is only this one eternal moment of Now.

3) You are one with Consciousness and Consciousness is One. The Oneness of consciousness is all that there is.

4) What you put out comes back. This is the Law of Attraction, Karma, Creation, and Manifestation all in one.

5) Everything changes except the first four Laws.

Bashar's advice aims to help humans understand they create their own reality and are responsible for what they manifest.

If you understand these Universal Laws, then you will see how there is no This or That, but truly This AND That in the Universe. Everything is here and now and everything is connected. All the contrast that you see between things is necessary for there to be the experience of reality.

Nothing exists without its opposite or other side of the spectrum. We could not know what anything is if we did not have contrast to delineate a thing. Contrast is the most powerful and necessary force in the Universe. Without it there would be no existence or experience of existence. We must have contrast to have experience. It's that simple.

As we acknowledge this, we can take it back into the context of the "Devil" and how he is our most necessary and greatest teacher of existence and reality. If we did not have the negative side of creation, we could not experience the positive side of creation. If we did not have this thing we call the "Devil" we could not know "God" or Heaven.

If we cannot accept our whole nature as a being of both light and dark, positive and negative, wanted and unwanted, we cannot fulfill our fullest potential here on the Earth Plane. We must face and integrate our Devil to become the fullest versions of creation that we were meant to be. God made us in its own likeness and image.

Why should we believe that God made a mistake with just us? Everything in the universe is a perfect creation of the creator…well, except for us. Somehow God made a mistake with us and created us flawed and bad and in need of fixing. REALLY?!

The only flaw we have is our ability to deny the perfection of our creation and the perfection of our wholeness. Your negative side is perfect just as it is and is a tool of contrast needed to help you decide what you prefer from what you don't. This tool is necessary and useful when properly used. You are not broken or bad, you have just been taught wrongly that you must deny a needed part of you to be a "Good Person."

As we've already explored, no one can tell you or decide for you whether you are a good person or a bad person except for you. You get to decide for yourself who and what you are for yourself and to the rest of the world. Your greatest power comes from your acceptance and utilization of all of you.

As the Heart-Math Institute states in its frequency studies, love was thought to be the highest frequency emotion for many, many years. Now they have evidence that Love, though a very high frequency emotion, is not the most powerful frequency a Human can emit.

New evidence now shows that Authenticity is anywhere from four times to 4,000 times more powerful than Love alone. When a person is being their full selves, they are the most powerful version of themselves they can be. Wouldn't we all like to be four to 4,000 percent more powerful in our lives? I know I would!

I've thought long and hard about this new discovery and have come to this conclusion. The reason authenticity is so much more powerful than love, is because Love, as we tend to define it, is an outward expression. We love others, we love nature, we love food, we love exercise, we love so many things outside ourselves. Our lives are full of the love of others and things outside of us.

Authenticity, on the other hand, is the truest love of self and expression of self-love there can be. We are loving ourselves enough to be our true authentic selves and that love directed internally is the most powerful thing we can do as Humans. Loving yourself enough to express yourself truly out into the world for others to see and experience is the greatest example of the creator's perfection there can be.

You are the most impactful, inspiring, and effective when you are being your truest authentic self. Just by being your most authentic and powerful self you make the greatest impact and give the greatest gift to all those you encounter and interact with. You are showing them that if you can be your authentic self, so can they. And when we are all being our authentic selves, we can create the world of our dreams and inspire everyone else to do the same.

You have not been wrong or bad your whole life, you've just not been being yourself. Most of us have been taught that being ourselves was vulnerability and vulnerability is weakness. Now we know different. Authenticity is strength and being your truest self is the greatest form of self-love and love towards the creator that we can give.

Now that you know the power of authenticity, let's dive into how we can peel back the layers and get to the core of your most authentic expression of self.

Chapter Nine

THE SHADOW & THE INNER CHILD

Welcome to my newest download and aha from spirit. It hit me recently that all this fighting the devil, subduing the shadow self, killing the Ego stuff; is really just different levels of inner child work.

Crazy, I know. But hear me out.

All this "SHADOW" work that I, and others, speak of as the secret path to your own wholeness and self-awareness has morphed for me recently and has taken on a whole new dimension that could simplify or complicate things, depending on how you take it on and utilize this information.

Let me start with my theory and we can go from there.

What hit me in the face like a ton of bricks recently, is this seemingly simple concept: All of our "Shadow" work is really just "Inner Child Work" in disguise. It is our unhealed inner child that is leading us into the dark realms of the Shadow Self. The same "Shadow-Side" that we are told we need to investigate, integrate and ultimately love and accept.

What I have noticed on my own personal journey, is that it seems much easier and more palatable to label this work "Inner Child Work" than to delve into the darkness of "Shadow Work." Duh Duhhh Dunnnnn… Cue spooky music!! The connotation of "Shadow Work" goes hand in hand with the belief that there is something intrinsically wrong with us. That somehow the creator made a mistake when making us and now we have to fix what is broken.

The issue, as usual, isn't the label or the name, but our constant dedication to avoiding anything dark and spooky, or that could diminish our already diminished sense of self. Most of us are so critical and hard on ourselves that the thought of delving into a Darkside of our mind and psyche tends to send most screaming back into their preferred delusion of self and numbing agent.

In this seemingly dualistic world of our perceptual existence, we believe in good and bad, light and dark, up and down, young and old, etc., etc., etc. However, that is all a matter of perspective and perceptual awareness.

I am not attempting to diminish your life struggles against "The Dark" in you, or your striving for the light and the goodness of the divine. On the contrary, I do believe I have found the ultimate loophole for all my wisdom seekers who are afraid of the dark.

Let me explain: What I propose is this.

Your unhealed, abandoned, neglected and traumatized Inner Child IS the source of all your "Shadow" and dark egoic behaviors. It IS that very traumatized child within each of us that sends us out into the world seeking soothing behaviors to deal and cope with all the unacknowledged aches and pains.

It is not so much that each of us has this EVIL DEVIL within that is battling to escape and take over and destroy our lives, but a small child desperate for attention and love, acting out in whatever way worked for them in childhood and continuing to act out in our "Adult" world because we have not had the knowledge or awareness to investigate, integrate and heal that inner child screaming for love and connection.

So, there you have it, in a nutshell, my concept, that I hope, will revolutionize the Shadow Work theology and help all my religious friends who fear "THE DEVIL," to continue with their healing work utilizing this Shadow Child Work concept.

Let's dig in and explore this concept a little more for all my mercurial friends who need more than an overview, but love examples that they can apply to their personal experience.

Your unhealed inner child acts out in so many unhealthy and traumatized ways, that it is a wonder we do as well as we do in the world today. The very coping mechanisms/behaviors that we used successfully as children to survive our childhoods, became the same Shadow Work subjects that we're all in therapy to address now.

Even though isolating and caretaking behaviors worked for us with our traumatized parents and kept us safe from hyper-criticism and punishment for being under foot or too visible. It is those coping mechanisms that are holding you back from your own unique personal expression and passions. What worked as an innocent and ignorant child, will never work as a responsible adult in the world today. This is why we, collectively, spend billions a year on therapy and healing modalities to "Work" on ourselves and improve what we see as our "Faults."

However, I'd like to propose that these behaviors aren't truly flaws or faults, but merely antiquated behaviors out of place in our adult world. As a matter of fact, I'd propose that these exact behaviors, when healed and integrated, lead to our own person SUPERPOWERS.

I'm a firm believer in the motto, "In Your Pain is your Purpose and Passion."

This concept is the true reason and inspiration for this book and for the work I do in the world. I would like to help as many people as possible to acknowledge and heal their inner little devils and find their own power and strength in integrating all parts, pieces and sides of the multi-faceted gem that we each are.

We have tried to "KILL THE EGO" and "DENY OUR LESSER IMPULSES," but how has that worked for us so far?

When we deny a part of ourselves, we deny the energy of that part and therefore do not allow that energy to flow in its necessary way. Energy must flow, and as we are all aware nowadays, everything is energy, especially our emotional coping behaviors. These behaviors are our way of dealing with and, in most cases, suppressing the energy of those emotions that just need acknowledgement and an outlet to flow through.

When we acknowledge, accept, investigate, integrate, understand and utilize those suppressed energies, we create the integration within ourselves that we have been lacking. This integration of all those parts and pieces of ourselves leads to our full authentic expression of self. Integration is the only path forward into the new world of awareness and enlightenment. Christ Consciousness is all about self-love and self-acceptance and none of that is possible without full self-awareness, acceptance and integration.

Facing The Devil in You is not a fiery battle to the death in the deepest darkest corner of Hell or Hades or your Psyche. It is unfiltered awareness and acceptance of all aspects of our multifaceted humanness. Without acceptance and integration, you will always be held back from acting in your full power by the weight of the anchors of your past self that you are ignoring as bad or less than.

In all the years of men's work that I have been a part of, I have found that it is the integrated man who is in his full power and capacity. His greatness lies in his ability to integrate the fearful, shameful, angry and violent parts of himself with the loving and nurturing parts of himself. Not as two disparate parts that must somehow be smashed together through brute force, but as two sides of his capacity to love and protect.

Every great man in history was capable of great violence and harm to others, if who and what they loved was threatened. It is not the passive man who is virtuous, but the dangerous man who has his dangerous side under control and utilizes that energy for good who contains virtue.

Passivity is not an absence of violence, but an absence of the ability to protect that which he values. A passive man has no resource when he is threatened with violence, but to submit and give up that which he values.

A man who is capable of true personal power and violence may be capable of harming others, but when he can keep that part of himself under control is capable of defending that which he values and loves when it is threatened by others without having to resort to violence. Most of the time, just the threat of violence is enough to end a conflict. It is the lack of a threat of power and violence that tends to exacerbate a conflict further.

"It is better to be a Warrior in a Garden, than a Gardener in a War." ~Miyamoto Musashi.

Within this concept lies the very same concept of healing and integrating the inner child that will access a man's greatness. When a man can access and integrate his inner child, he finds the aspects of himself that he may have been missing as an adult in the world. His many failings can be traced directly back to the unhealed inner child within him.

A man's fear of rejection comes from his past childhood reality, that led to a perceived inner reality of a lack of support, or a lack of feeling supported in the world. That part of him will do everything it can to keep him safe from rejection and belittlement. The traumatized inner child doesn't know that avoiding those things will hinder his ability to succeed in the world today. As far as that part of him is concerned, he is still six years old and vulnerable to the same harm as his six-year-old self. There is no awareness of the passage of time, capability or experience for the inner child portion of him that is trying to protect him.

That protective inner child will turn into the very DEVIL that he fears to face, because he lacks understanding of the Inner Child and its loving attempts to protect him from himself. It is the grown man's job and responsibility to uncover that inner child portion of himself. To heal it, re-raise it and shift it from protective mode back into living mode. Living Mode would be the mode of fearless self-expression that was lost back in childhood when the original trauma happened.

There are many modalities today that offer inner child work. One of my favorites is: Internal Family System. Internal Family System helps us to acknowledge those exiled parts of ourselves that are trying to protect, manage and care for our adult selves in the many and varied unhealthy ways that ultimately turn into the Devils we fear to face within us.

Facing the Devil in You is truly the best way to the true freedom of self that we are all wishing to obtain in our lives. Every man I know is fighting a silent battle to come to terms with the Devil he feels within himself.

He feels less than, broken, and worthless because he thinks there is a disparate part of him that hates him and is constantly trying to sabotage all his efforts to be something in the world.

I can speak firsthand about this internal battle most of us deal with on a daily basis. I know the depression that ensues from not understanding why we self-sabotage, why we won't just "Do It," why we won't face our fears and make something out of ourselves, why we will only allow ourselves to go just so far, but no further.

It is this protective inner child within us that becomes the Devil we must face to obtain our personal freedom and power in the world.

Thankfully, it is much easier to do the work when you understand that you are not fighting "The Devil" inside you, but healing and re-parenting the child within you into the man you've always wanted and knew you could be.

I've found in my own healing journey, that as soon as I understood it was the inner child part of me causing all the problems I saw in my life, it was simple to accept that part as the innocent little child that needed love and attention from me. We as adults can accept so much more from children than we can from ourselves or other adults. Acknowledging and accepting that the part of us acting out and causing all the issues is just an innocent and ignorant child within us doing the best it can to deal with adult issues that it was never prepared to deal with.

I can accept temper tantrums, angry outbursts and all sorts of bad behavior from a child that I would never accept from an adult person. Yet, when we realize that all the acting-out adults we see in the world are just being run by their inner children acting out desperate for love and attention. Hell, if we could see our romantic partners in this same light, it would be so much easier to treat them with love and kindness when their inner child acts out, than to judge and demean them like we usually do as "Adults in Relationship."

The best way to gain patience and perspective with another is to gain the same patience and perspective with yourself. The inner child work you do for yourself will directly translate to how you treat and deal with others in your life. Once you can accept and love the inner child in you, then you can also accept and love the inner child in others.

The most angry, confrontational and unpleasant person you've ever dealt with is just a person being run by their traumatized inner child desperate for the same love and attention we are all craving. You don't have to take it on yourself to try to heal the whole world with your newly acquired knowledge, but starting in your own home will lead to the very world change we all would like to see.

Heal your own inner child and love all others still in the process of growth and healing. Help those who you feel drawn to help, if and only if, they ask for help. Be the example of a healed person for others to see and you will do your part in inspiring their own work on themselves.

You being a healed, grounded and loving person is the best medicine and service you could give to the rest of the world. Your example will create the ripples of change you wish to bring to the world. No need to hold a meeting and scream from the mountaintops. Just be your most powerful authentic self out in the world and you will be doing your work to change the world for the better. Your example is all that's required for you to change the world.

Now, if you feel so called to do more and be more in the world, then follow that intuition and gut feeling. I cannot and will not tell you what to do with your life. Who am I to tell you or anyone else what they should do? You will know what to do by following your own heart. Let no one else tell you what to do either.

Chapter Ten

THE DEVIL IS IN THE DETAILS

"Thoughts are Things and they have a Home deep within you."

This chapter will be the 'Practical Application' chapter and give you everything you need to start working with your shadow side and inner child today. Because NOW is all we have when it comes to personal development and self betterment.

AS THE WISE MAN SAID; "IF NOT NOW, WHEN?"

What we have to take into account as we begin this journey of self discovery is this: your shadow and inner child are not locked away or some distant aspect of you... They are as close as your own thoughts... As a matter of fact, they are the source of most of your thoughts.

That inner voice that nags, the inner critic, the overly people pleasing, boundary making, rule needing, fearful, catastrophising, self-deprecating, self-critical part of your mind comes from your inner child self attempting to

147

protect itself and you from further harm and to safely fit in. It is those ingrained patterns of thought we must first address and work on accepting and integrating to begin the Facing the Devil in You process.

Each one of those voices in your head that is attempting to protect you in its own unique way, is the voice of your inner Devil, Shadow, and inner child. For many of us those voices sound like our overly critical father or catastrophising mother, but they are only the mask our own inner voice likes to take. Each voice in our head is related to another part of us that is doing its best to keep us alive and safe. The problems arise when we constantly believe those inner voices and never question them or their motives.

Every negative thought in your head comes from somewhere inside you. A lesson learned from your parents or guardians. Maybe something you picked up on the streets of your neighborhood. Or, oftentimes, the stories we make up ourselves as children when faced with situations we were not prepared for or meant to handle on our own.

Each arguing voice in your head relates to a part of you doing its best to protect you. The problem being, they do not talk to each other and come to a consensus on how best to do that. We each have an entire 'Families' worth of parts and pieces wanting to keep us safe from the big bad world in its own way. If you stop to examine your own mind for a minute, you'll see what I mean.

You have the one voice telling you to be careful and not get too big for your britches, alongside another voice screaming about how unfair the world is and how you can never catch a break, next to the quiet small voice of your little self that just wants to make friends and have some fun for a change. And, lest we forget, the overpowering voice of self-criticism trying to keep you small and safe, while your conscious mind attempts to get you to grow bigger and better to gain more exposure and impact on the world.

These voices fight amongst each other and with your conscious mind to attempt to guide you towards safety and survival. And, well, you're still here, so they're succeeding. But, to what detriment of your aspirations and dreams?

The most diabolical issue of your inner voices and thoughts, is that they will fight to protect themselves from you and your desire to change them. You can say all the positive affirmations you want a hundred times a day, but if you do not dig down into the dirt of your psyche to pull those thoughts up by the root, they will fester and grow anew within you. Do not allow the weeds of negativity in your own mind sprout to take over the garden of positive thoughts and feelings you have fought so hard to create.

This process falls into what I like to call, 'The Twelve Step Two-Step'. All coaching and therapies like Neuro Linguistic Programming, or NLP, and Internal Family System, or IFS treatments fall into the category of the 'Twelve Step Two-Step'. By this I mean, each has a series of steps to follow and within those steps there is usually a step back or two to contend with. However, in my humble opinion, those step backs are the most important and impactful parts of the systems, because it is in the step back that you start to become aware of your own patternings and habits of behavior, thoughts and actions.

The more you have your step backs in whatever system you are using, the more aware you will become of your habitual patterns. The more aware you become of them, the sooner and sooner you can notice, address and change those thoughts and patterns. Each time you have a step back, where you fall back into an old habit or thought pattern, do not beat yourself up and assume failure. Rejoice in your step back and know it is the most vital part of the process of self-healing and self-awareness.

As the saying goes, 'We're only as sick as our secrets', and your step backs will highlight those secrets you were trying to hide from yourself. We all do it. We all hide those parts of ourselves we think are bad or dirty or even just weird from the rest of the world… Or so we think.

In actuality, all those skeletons in the closet that we wish to hide from the world, can be pretty obvious to those who truly care about us enough to know us on a deep personal level. They see all our little pic-a-dillows we wish to keep from them. As a matter of fact, the harder we try to hide our shame from others, the easier they are to see.

No, no one can read your mind and no, they don't know all the crazy thoughts you have in your head. But, they can feel your energy, see your expressions and witness how you act. Which, to anyone paying attention, is pretty much the same thing as telepathy. So, take yourself off the hook of hiding everything from those that love you. They probably already know and still love you anyway.

As a matter of fact, letting your loved ones know what you are doing and why, will give you several allies in your process of Facing the Devil in You. They can be your greatest mirrors and coaches, helping you to see your blind spots you weren't aware of, as well as, the amazing parts of you that you can't or won't see about yourself due to all those negative voices in your head.

Here's the first step to begin up your staircase of self-awareness and self-love: Watch your thoughts and share them with those you love and who love you.

When we are brave enough to share our thoughts with our loved ones, (or a coach or counselor if you're not ready to unload on those closest to you), you take those deep dark thoughts out of the shadows and expose them to the light of consciousness. Once exposed to the light, they are no longer secrets and can be examined for legitimacy and relevance to you and your future goals.

You will find, during this light shedding process, that we all think a lot of stupid bullshit about ourselves and others all day long. The hidden parts of us that are creating most of our thoughts and habits, are some of the worst judges of character, reality and others. They are the most reactionary and ignorant parts of us, because those parts are still 4, 5 and 6 year olds within us attempting to make adult decisions for our safety, survival and future. DO NOT TRUST THEM!!

As you examine your thoughts and find those persistent, pervasive and rebellious thoughts who fight for their own survival despite your best efforts to change them into positive thoughts, know that it is time to go deeper. Dig down into your shadow side and see which inner child part of you is still trying to protect you from the big bad world by using those negative thoughts and help set them free by shedding light on them, their method of protection and how it isn't actually accomplishing the results they are hoping for. As you reeducate those inner child parts of you, you can set them free from the roles they adopted far too young in an attempt to protect themselves and you. They never wanted that job and only did it because they thought it was the only way to protect you from being hurt again.

As adults today we all have many, many hidden parts of ourselves that are running the majority of our thoughts and behaviors independent of our grown adult conscious minds. When you realize this, you can easily see why it seems like we have a bunch of 8 year old kids in adult bodies pretending they're normal and ok to fit in with society and find safety.

I'm hoping this is all making a kind of sense to you and that you are feeling inspired to do some inner thought exploration with me. If this is the case, let's get into some steps and practices.

STEP 1: BREATHE AND ACKNOWLEDGE YOUR THOUGHT/S.

When we have these negative thoughts about ourselves, we need to stop, take a breath and acknowledge that we just had that hateful and detrimental thought. Acknowledge the thought without judgment or self-criticism. Just look at it like you would a small child having a temper tantrum or negative reaction. Because, that's where the thought is coming from.

Your unhealed child part is reacting to a situation it doesn't have the tools to deal with. Acknowledge and thank that inner child part of you for trying to protect you and keep you safe in the only way it knows how to. Tell them you have it from here and they can go back to playing now. Set your inner child free and you'll release that thought and behavior matrix from your system.

~Remember, you are not your thoughts. You are the one observing your thoughts and can be outside their influence, if you so choose to be. You are the master of your reality and your thoughts are your alchemical ingredients. This concept may be easy to grasp intellectually, but can be harder to believe and implement as you begin.~

STEP 2: LEARN ABOUT YOUR COMMON THOUGHTS AND REACTIONS THROUGH DETACHED OBSERVATION.

This step may take some time and effort to master, due to our propensity to judge and demean any part of ourselves we don't approve of or appreciate. It's hard to not react negatively when that same stupid thought pops into your head.

The Twelve Step Two-step is all about noticing those thoughts and then noticing them again as they pop up. Each time you notice the thought, you'll notice it sooner than the last time, and you'll get to a point when you will catch yourself about to have that thought and you'll decide not to. That's when you know you've successfully completed the Twelve Step Two-Step... On that thought.

You will continue this process until you reach such a level of enlightenment that, like the Dalai Lama and maybe Eckart Tolle, you no longer have any negative self-talk thoughts.

STEP 3: LEARN TO LOVE YOUR INNER CHILD

What I have found extremely helpful in this process is to constantly remind myself and remember that I am re-parenting the little Me inside myself. When addressing my negative thoughts and reactions, acknowledging that those thoughts and reactions are those of a small child doing its very best to protect itself from trauma, harm, danger, and ostracization from the family/group.

Children are extremely adaptable and resilient in the face of trauma and abuse. However, their tools of adaptation as a child do not translate well into the adult world. Which begins to make a lot of sense when you observe your so-called 'Adult' world and see everyone running around acting like it's "Lord of The Flies" out there. The whole world is just a bunch of children in adult costumes screaming about 'It's Not Fair' and 'I'm taking my ball and going home'.

Your thoughts come from the deepest parts of you and will be your guide back to those parts. Each thought of fear and judgment comes from that exiled inner child part of you that wants to stop the bad things from happening again.

Acknowledge your thoughts, examine them and follow them back to the little one inside you that needs your love and attention to heal. Your thoughts are not you. You are the observer of your thoughts and if you are the observer, then you are not the thought. Your observation and examination will show you the legitimacy or falsity of your thoughts. Thereby giving you the power to change them and reprogram your mind for success and health.

STEP 4: SELF THERAPY

This is the part of therapy, self-analysis and self-discovery that trips most of us up and can take the longest time due to the personal nature of our thoughts. Most of us believe our thoughts are us and that what we think must be true because we are thinking it. But, when you take the deep dive into thought examination, you'll see that the majority of our thoughts come from someone else and are recycled daily.

If you follow any of Dr. Joe Dispenza's work you'll have heard him talk about us running on autopilot and having the same sets of thoughts everyday. Basically living in a 'Groundhog's Day' type of existence. If you think the same thoughts every day and do the same things everyday, then you are not living your life, you are repeating a pattern. And, old patterns are not going to get you anything new. You have the same old thoughts and same old experiences everyday because you are running the same patterns every day.

It is time to take a stand and make a decision to create something new. New is scary! New is uncomfortable! New is unknown! But, New is also exciting, invigorating, inspiring, creative, magical and outside your old same old-same old pattern of life.

Follow your thoughts down the Rabbit Hole of you and free your exiles from their prison of bondage and servitude to an old paradigm of thoughts and actions that no longer serves you and holds you back from all the new and wonder your life has to offer. Your life is your own magical creation. You just have to free your mind and get comfortable being uncomfortable for the New to flow in.

You are at the controls of your next chapter, and with a little work and investigation that 'New Chapter' can actually be new, and not a rerun of the same old-same old you've been experiencing so far.

STEP 5: LEAN INTO THE DISCOMFORT

Yes, I know it's scary and unfamiliar and not what you're used to, but I can imagine, you are tired of what you're used to and ready for something new in your life. New is possible and at your fingertips, you just have to turn inward and begin your self-love journey back to wholeness and self-acceptance.

If you have ever received a hug from a small child when they are full of love or scared to death and hanging on to you for dear life, and you've felt the heart swelling, heart-breaking love that comes to you in that moment; then you already know what awaits you when you free your exiled inner child and bring them back into integration with you.

Imagine it for a moment. You can have the same amazing heart-opening feeling you get from hugging your children, from inside you. No one else needs to be involved. You can hug, calm, and sooth yourself as you would a small child. You can give yourself the love and attention you have been missing from your family, relationships, and the world. You have the power to be your own parent, loved one, lover, coach, therapist, elder, mentor, etc…

Just like the 'Hot Tub Analogy', it will be intense and uncomfortable at first. Just breathe and settle in. Soon you will get used to it and then begin to revel in it. As you settle into the Hot Tub of self-awareness you will find the Collateral Beauty in your Inner Child's Pain and learn to love it as you have learned to love so many other things and people.

The Collateral Beauty in the pain of life is this, it is all based in Love and when you can sit with it and get past the initial pain and discomfort, you will find the Love beneath and know you are not alone, broken, bad, unworthy, worthless, ugly, unwanted or unnecessary. You are a priceless spark of the Creator and the Universe could not be the Universe without you. You are critical, precious and needed for all the rest of life to exist and progress. NO PRESSURE!

On a final note; when it comes to your thoughts, be prepared for push back, resistance, and fighting from your thoughts. Your thoughts will fight for their survival, especially the negative thoughts. The negative thoughts tend to be the most ingrained and hard to overcome, due to their ingrained purpose of protection. They believe they are protecting you from the 'Big Bad World'. Expect this resistance and fight from your thoughts and you will not be surprised when it happens.

I find that it is easier to work with healing your inner child parts and re-integrating them, than it is to attempt to change every little thought one at a time. Healing the wounded inner child part that has been exiled away from the whole Self will have a greater effect in changing the majority of your survival and negative thoughts.

The 'Self' or the 'Greater Self' is the greater part of you that is the observer of your thoughts, moods and actions. This is the part that you will be re-integrating your Exiles with. This is the true you and the part of you that has the energy and power to handle all the Managers, Firefighters, and Exiles within you.

To tap into your 'Greater Self' I suggest meditation, time in nature, reflection, journaling, and maybe even sensory deprivation to get you acquainted with the larger part of you outside of your incessant thoughts, moods, and reactions to the world around you.

You will know when you connect with your Greater Self when you find peace in the present moment and know that all is well and that all this is temporary and not as big a deal as we tend to think it is. Inner Peace comes from presence, stillness and connection with the Greater Self. The more you can return to this connection with your Greater Self, the happier you will be.

As your journey of Facing the Devil in You continues, feel free to begin to practice watching, acknowledging and investigating your thoughts. The more you practice the better you will get.

Start by asking these questions when you have thoughts you do not prefer:

(INQUIRY QUESTIONS FROM BYRON KATIE'S 'THE WORK')

#1: Is this thought true?

#2: Is there any possible way that this thought could not be true?

#3: How do I feel when I think that thought?

#4: Who would I be if I could not think that thought?

The Inquiry Process, developed by Byron Katie, is a powerful way to add space between you and your thoughts and to give you the tools to question and investigate the thoughts in your head.

I would highly recommend learning more about Byron Katie and her powerful work at: **www.TheWork.com**

Chapter Eleven

DANCING WITH YOUR *DEVIL*...

H ave you come to terms with your inner *DEVIL* yet? Or are you still fighting within yourself over the term: *DEVIL?*

That's fair and, honestly, to be expected. No one wants to admit that there is a part of them that isn't what they want it to be. It takes great courage and humility to accept those parts of ourselves we aren't thrilled with or want to expose to others. The fear of self-judgment is a huge pill to swallow. But the fear of other people's judgment is an even harder pill to swallow. Especially the judgment from those we love and rely on.

What will they think? What will they do when they find out? Will they leave me as I fear they will? Will they condemn me as wrong, broken or not worthy? Will they verify all those inner fears we hold about ourselves? Those very same fears we are desperate to hide and ignore when they come to the surface.

Do not feel ashamed of those fears. Do not feel less than because you have them. If everyone acknowledged and shared those fears together, we would see how alike we all are and realize it is in the sharing of our deepest, darkest fears that we find the most connection and common ground.

As an extra benefit to sharing these fears with those you love and deem safe enough and responsible enough to share with, you'll have less fear of what those BIG BAD OTHERS will think if they find out. Once your family and loved ones know your fears and love and accept you even more for sharing them. You will develop a stronger sense of self and a greater resilience for the judgment of others, because you'll realize their judgment doesn't matter a lick, when the people in your life who do matter accept you just as you are. Not in spite of your flaws and fears, but because of them.

SO... What do we do with our Devils?

Well, not to put too fine a point on it, but we have to follow the formula.

THE INTERNAL DEVIL INTEGRATION FORMULA GOES SOMETHING LIKE THIS...

Step 1: Acknowledge Your Inner Devil/Shadow/Child
Step 2: Accept that you have said part of yourself.

Step 3: Investigate those parts to find out how they formed, how they are trying to protect you, and how you can let them off the hook of trying to protect the Adult You.

Step 4: Understand and integrate each of the parts of you.

Step 5: Utilize those parts to connect and empathize with all the others in your life who have similar parts and pieces within them.

Simple, right? Just 5 simple steps to becoming the biggest and best version of yourself.

Well, yes and no...

I would advise you to seek help and support during this process. You'll want to find a professional therapist to witness and walk you through this process. If you can't afford a therapist or just don't want to go to one at this point, then find someone who you know and trust who has already used the formula and completed the integration process.

Experience is the best teacher and a friend who has already been there will understand what you are going through and be able to hold space for you as you investigate and integrate these parts of you.

If you are able to find a therapist and want to go that route, let them know what you are doing and why. As this is a newer method of integration and not widely known or used, your therapist may or may not be on board with it.

If you're not sure where to start, I'd suggest researching and finding an "Internal Family System" therapist to start with. That work is very similar to this work and inspired much of this process.

I utilized "Internal Family System" therapy in my own life to great effect. This system has a reported 80% effectiveness rate and can help any of you who are ready for greater self-awareness, acceptance and personal growth.

I am such a fan of IFS, that I have gotten my IFS certification so that I can utilize this effective system in my own practice as a coach and counselor.

Now that I have promoted and plugged IFS, let me get back to those of you who, like me, tend to go the Do-It-Yourself route. There is nothing saying you cannot do this work on your own. However, you will find greater and faster results with help.

That being said, I understand the desire to find the proof in the pudding, as it were. You want to give it a try and see what results you get for yourself before committing to a more in-depth process. All to the good and as long as you are doing something you are making progress in the right direction.

In the next few chapters I will break down the Formula step by step with personal examples from my life and others' experiences in the work to help you with your own process.

The *Devil* in you is not the nightmarish monster of your childhood. It is no more a bogeyman than the shadows in your closet are. Your inner *Devil* will become your best friend and greatest ally once you complete the formula and integrate this most loving part into the new whole you.

Do not run from your *Devil.* Do not hide from your *Devil.* Acknowledge your *Devil,* accept your *Devil,* investigate your *Devil,* understand and integrate your *Devil,* and utilize your *Devil* to strengthen and empower your life moving forward.

Are you ready? Let's get to work!

Chapter Twelve

ACKNOWLEDGE AND ACCEPT

First and foremost, I want to assuage any doubts you may have about the value and validity of this exercise. The "DEVIL" is nothing more than the unexplored parts of our inner selves that may be hidden away due to a lack of awareness or maturity to deal with certain events in our formative years.

It is not some evil entity hungry for your soul, no matter how much it may feel like it is. The evil being within you is just a part of your younger mind that is doing it's very best to keep you safe and whole. It just doesn't have the knowledge, wisdom or tools to properly protect you in a healthy and sustainable way. Like most children have a tendency to do, it over-reacted and turned that over-reaction into a habitual tool of protection.

Thus, you may find it seems daunting to address this part of you that feels so intrinsic to your personality. I know it did for me. Let me assure you that it is much easier than you may think to acknowledge and accept this part of yourself when you put it into the proper context.

Perspective in life is the lens through which we see and create the world we experience. It is just that most of us have a skewed perspective due to some false logic we adopted as children. If Dad was mad at us, we assumed we were bad in some fundamental way and consciously or unconsciously decided to hide our "Badness" and make sure to never make Dad mad again.

However, if you use a small amount of mature logical thinking, you'll quickly see how faulty that decision would be. Dad wasn't really mad at you or saying you were intrinsically bad. Dad was stressed out and reacted badly to you in a moment of weakness that you took to mean something about you that it never did. Therefore, your subconscious operating system is using a faulty logic gate to keep you safe and secure.

The *Devil* in you that is "ruining your life" and "sabotaging all your efforts to succeed" is just a younger version of you doing the best it can to keep you safe and your inner version of Dad happy with you.

If like mine, your father is no longer in the physical realm, then you are operating on a faulty and outdated logic sequence to run your life. Who is it you are trying to appease and make happy if your father, whom you created this behavior for, is no longer in the picture? You cannot blame him anymore for your actions, behaviors and beliefs if he is no longer in the picture. You are the adult now and you have the capacity to heal and change your behaviors for the better. If not you, then who?

As we begin the acknowledgment process, I ask for you to view these behaviors and patterns that represent the *DEVIL* you need to face, as just the misguided protection of your younger less mature self. Let's use love and appreciation for all the hard work of keeping you safe and secure to help release this part of you from their exiled state and welcome them back into the fold of the whole you.

I'll utilize and reference the Inner Family System work in these chapters. For those of you who find these chapters helpful and applicable to your life and who would like to apply these techniques into your life and practice, please go to www.ifs-institute.com to learn more about this system of integrative therapy.

Here is a brief overview of IFS:

Within all of us is a whole family dynamic of parts and pieces of our personalities working tirelessly to keep you safe from past traumas and harm. When a traumatic event happens to us as children, we tend to break off that piece of us that was traumatized and hide it away for safe-keeping. That part becomes the "Exiled Part" of us that is hidden in a dark corner of our psyche and protected from further trauma by other parts of us. Those other parts of us, that take up the job of protecting that exiled part we'll call "Managers" and "Fire Fighters." These parts start to manage us away from those traumatic triggers and to soothe the pain of those triggers.

It is these "Managers" and "Fire Fighters" parts of us that are trying their very best to protect that "Exiled Part" of us that cause the greatest problems of self-sabotage and feelings of "I Can't" within us, because of the fear of further trauma.

When these events happened to us as children, they were not at all anything we might consider traumatic or even worth paying attention to today. Now that we are older, more experienced and wiser, we can handle those traumas and heal the Exiled Parts back into homeostasis and reintegrate them.

The feelings of unworthiness, not good enough-ness, brokenness or what we see as flaws in ourselves, stem from theses exiled parts that have not been reintegrated back into the greater whole of our persona. The reason we feel these unhelpful feelings is to keep us safe from gaining too much attention and thereby being judged by others or attempting to achieve goals and possibly experiencing failure. In other people's experience, these parts keep you so busy achieving goals, that you have no time to stop and feel or think about the feelings within you. Others cope through addictive behaviors that serve the same purpose of distraction and soothing you away from feeling the pain inside. These addictive behaviors can show up as shopping, working out, controlling behavior, attention seeking, social media influencers, body dysmorphia, alcohol, drugs, diet, mental health issues, and many other things.

Out of a deep love and desire to protect our internal little selves, we create walls, boxes, behaviors and beliefs to stop us from experiencing the traumas of our past childhood. When you begin to dig into your self-sabotaging behaviors with this mindset, you release the desire or need to demean, judge or punish yourself. You can see that underneath all the negative behaviors that you previously judged, is love of self and a desire to protect.

Just as grief is a fact of life, most of us do not sit with the pain of grief nor explore what is underneath it to get to the Deep Love and Beauty at its core. If you did not Love deeply and appreciate those that you lost, you would not and could not grieve for them. Grief is one of the most beautiful human experiences, when we can see it from the perspective of the great love at the core.

PRACTICAL APPLICATION TO GAIN ACKNOWLEDGEMENT AND ACCEPTANCE OF YOUR INNER EXILES.

Step 1: Feel what you are feeling. Do not run from it or try to stuff it or soothe it with chemicals. Feel the feelings. Look them straight in the eye without fear.

You are not looking into the face of the horned demon. You are looking into the eyes of your younger self who didn't know a better way to protect you.

I call this step the Hot Tub Step, because it can be really intense in the beginning, but the longer you breathe into it and sit with it, the more comfortable the feeling becomes. The longer you sit with it the more you release the love hiding within the pain and the more pleasurable that feeling can and will become for you.

I had this experience of "Collateral Beauty" during one of my past heartbreaks at the end of relationship. As I sat in my car crying my eyes out and breathing deeply, I got to a point when my heart opened, and I felt the love blooming up out of the pain. The heartbreak was because of the love that was built in the relationship. The breaking of the relationship was in a way, the breaking of the love. But even in the pain of loss, love is still the core of the feelings.

Love is all there is and what everything is made of. Fear is just the lack of love, or the opposite end of the spectrum of love. Your inner traumas that we will dig into are still made of love. At their core they are love, love that has been covered in fear and pain. This realization will help you process your feelings more easily when you understand that the finish line is love.

Step 2: Acknowledge that part of you for trying to protect you and thank it for all its hard work. Let your exiled part know that you are older now, an adult, and you can now handle what it could not and is trying to protect you from. Acknowledge the pain, sit with it and give it the attention you needed when you were younger and received this shock to your system.

You can create a dialogue with your exiled part and find out how old it thinks you are. Usually, it will think you are still three, four, or five years old, the age you were when the trauma happened. You can tell it your current age and that you are grown now and capable of taking care of yourself. Reassure your younger part of your "Grown-up-ness" and that it can let go and stop holding up all the weight of the trauma.

Step 3: Luckily for you, once you acknowledge your exiled part, many will naturally gain acceptance of this part. However, some of you may not be ready to accept your exiled part after you've acknowledged it. This is to be expected at first. It isn't easy to just go from ignorance, to awareness, and straight to acceptance.

Acceptance isn't about approving of or making right those inner parts of you that you are now discovering. Acceptance is dropping the resistance to and judgment of those parts you have uncovered. Acceptance comes after acknowledgment because once you are aware of something you can no longer deny it, unless you want to delude yourself and deny its existence. This will cause a greater problem of cognitive dissonance and self-recrimination.

I would advise against that, if at all possible. You have enough to be getting on with doing this work, without hindering your hard-won progress by not accepting what is. There is a part of you that was exiled and needs your attention and love. Just like when you have a child, there is no going back or wishing it away. Only acceptance, love and attention for that child will do. You now have the opportunity to give the love, attention and acceptance to yourself that you didn't receive as a child.

Be honored and grateful for the chance to accept this part of you that was locked away for so long. Your growth, self-love, and happiness is dependent upon your acceptance of this inner child part of you and once you achieve acceptance, you will unlock the magic within you that was lost in your childhood.

Step 4: Once you have come to acceptance of your inner exile you are ready to let that exiled part out of its cage and set it free to go back to being its original self. Once you set your exiled part free, you can begin the work of reintegration.

Reintegration comes naturally on the heels of acceptance. Accepting your exiled parts will free them to come back into the fold of the greater You. Reintegration means freeing that part from its former cage and reinstating it into its former role within you. Most of our exiled parts that have been causing all the issues in our adult lives, had a very different job prior to the trauma that caused their exile-ment.

Once your part is reintegrated, you will find a long-lost part of you is now back and craving attention and freedom of expression. For all of us who were once gregarious and out-going children, who morphed into these "good little boys and girls" that were seen and not heard to appease the adults around us and thereby became reserved and timid when it was time to express ourselves. Thankfully, after the integration process, you will find a greater range of self-expression and far less timidity.

All our exiled parts want is to be back as a part of us and to be able to express their unique gifts and talents. To be able to be creative, imaginative and playful again. All those amazing parts of ourselves that we shut down, locked away and hide from the world, will now resurface and you have only to give it the opportunity to express itself to find that part of you that you've been missing for so many years.

Get ready for that inner child part of you to start popping up randomly and expressing joy, wonder, and excitement like you haven't experienced since your childhood. Have patience and grace with yourself as you relearn how to express yourself again freely.

Step 5: Managing Managers and Fire Fighters. Those parts of you that have been in charge of protecting that Exiled part of you will put up a fight when you start the acknowledgement and acceptance process. They have spent all these years since your childhood keeping that part locked away and protected from further harm and trauma.

It is a good idea, especially when you first begin this process, to find a certified Internal Family System practitioner to guide you. Once you've successfully reintegrated several Exiles with their support, then you may be able to start your own self integration processes.

Those Managers and Fire Fighters are to be approached and acknowledged in the same way as your Exiles. They have been operating out of love and a desire to protect. They are not malicious or evil demons inhabiting your mind. No matter how destructive the managing or firefighting behaviors, i.e.: drinking, drug abuse, sex addiction, shopping addiction, codependency or any of the myriad other addictive managing or soothing behaviors you've exhibited in the past. These parts were just trying to love and protect you in their own misguided ways.

Just like your exiled parts, your managers and firefighters didn't start off in those roles. They all had very different functions in your childhood years. But once the trauma happened, they adopted these new roles and have been faithfully fulfilling those roles ever since.

You now have the opportunity to set them free as well and return them back to their original functions from childhood. These managers and firefighters were once creative, imaginative, fun-loving aspects of you, prior to them taking on their newer functions as a manager or firefighter. As you begin to set them free, be prepared for greater levels of creativity, imagination, joy, and fun to come from and through you.

Step 6: Repeat. Repeat. Repeat. Repeat this process as often as needed and as frequently as feasible for your current life situations.

You'll find as you begin this journey of discovery into your internal universe that each discovery of a new exiled part will fill in the parts of you that you've been unconsciously missing that made you feel less than whole and complete.

Just be sure to consult an IFS professional during this process and allow them to be your second set of eyes.

They will be able to highlight your blind spots and be a valuable ally in helping you deal with your Managers, Firefighters, and Exiles.

Chapter Thirteen

INVESTIGATION & INTEGRATION

Investigation & Integration may seem similar to acknowledgement and acceptance, and you would be right to think so. However, these steps help to really get to the core of the reason why your Exiles were created in the first place and help you to know the reasons why you have been acting the way you have all your adult life.

Some of you will no doubt want to pass right over this chapter because you have that enviable talent of acceptance that many of the rest of us lack. You don't really care much about the hows or whys, but only about the efficiency of the technique. If this is you, feel free to skip this chapter if you're in a hurry.

However, if you aren't in a hurry, I would suggest investigating at least the first one or two of your exiles, to give you greater clarity and awareness around what created them in the first place. Many times, the traumas fall into similar categories and may even have a resonant theme. Understanding this will only help you with faster integration in the future as you continue with the process of Facing the Devil in You.

Investigation is one of those words that probably bring up an image of *Law & Order* or Sherlock Holmes or Columbo into your mind, depending on your age and upbringing. And, if you would like to put on your inner Sherlock Holmes hat and pipe to begin your internal investigations, by all means, go for it.

In many ways, investigation is investigation. We want to find out the whats, whys, and hows of the thing, and in that way, this form of investigation is the same. The main difference is that we are not investigating to assign guilt or wrongdoing. There is no bad guy to collar or Ego to kill in this work.

Our investigation should be performed with love and appreciation as we dig into the source of our "negative" behaviors and beliefs. I put negative in quotes, because as you investigate, you'll find that even though the outcome of the behaviors had unwanted effects in your adult life, those same behaviors had the desired effects for us as children. The only issue being that we aren't those same children anymore and what worked then, doesn't work for us today.

As you practiced Acknowledgement and Acceptance from the last chapter, you may have begun to see a pattern that relates directly to your current adult struggles of self-sabotage and self-worth. It is these patterns that we want to investigate further.

The reason you want to investigate further into those patterns is so that you may gain a greater understanding of yourselves and the patterning of your lives. When you understand fully your patterns and the whys behind them, you are better able to express yourself to your loved ones and are better able to educate them about your past behaviors and in that way, let them off the hook.

So many of us struggle in relationships, not because we are unworthy or unlovable, but because we do not have the awareness or vocabulary to express what is going on inside of us to our loved ones. Without that awareness, we are left a victim to our unconscious behaviors and belief systems that run us and our reactions to the world.

Investigating your unconscious drives and beliefs will more quickly free you and set you up for success than anything else I am currently aware of. You are an amazing creation of God and the only thing holding you back is your uninvestigated childhood trauma responses that became habits.

You have already begun the investigation process by following the steps in the last chapter. Now, you will need to exercise and bit more patience and curiosity than you needed to in the acknowledgement and acceptance steps.

Become your own personal detective and dig into all the little details of your past traumas and subsequent habitual behaviors that stemmed from that traumatic event. Learn what the event was and see that it is something you could easily handle now as an adult. Take over the responsibility of dealing with that event from your inner child self and free that part up to go back to its original function of fun, play, and imagination.

When you have investigated enough and feel you have all the pertinent information you need to understand your past and the subsequent behaviors that derived from those events. You are ready to integrate.

Integration, like acceptance, follows easily after investigation, if you are open to and willing to allow the information you gained to become a part of you. As long as you don't resist what you find in your investigation, you will naturally begin to integrate the information.

Most of you will find great relief during this process as you discover the whys behind your past unconscious behaviors and habits. You'll feel emancipated and freed up to be who you truly are in more areas of life.

I know in my own journey, when I learned more about why I acted the way I did and where that came from, I felt freed up and vindicated in many ways. Now I had an explanation. The reason why this freed me up is that I no longer felt broken or flawed. I felt a greater understanding and acceptance that I could lean on and utilize to explain to myself and others my past behaviors and habits as I made the steps to change them.

Chapter Fourteen

UNDERSTANDING & UTILIZING

Now that you have Acknowledged and Accepted, Investigated and Integrated your inner child, shadow and Devil, you are ready to move into Understanding and Utilization of those parts of yourself.

This part of the healing process is the most impactful and important because it gets you closer to your natural wholistic nature and gives you that many more tools to use in the creation of your unique life. When you have gotten this far into the healing process, you can see how those parts you were so afraid of and hiding from the world are the very parts that will empower you and lead to your greatest strengths and creations in the future.

Ignorance may be bliss, but understanding and utilization are the fuel to the fire of your power, purpose, and manifestations. Not to mention, the self-love and self-respect that naturally comes from this integrative healing process. We are better humans when we have all parts of ourselves at our disposal.

This chapter will be far shorter than the last few, due to the natural flow of acknowledgment to acceptance, acceptance to investigation, investigation to integration. Integration naturally flows into a greater understanding of those parts and that understanding naturally flows into utilization of your newly rediscovered parts.

When you went from crawling to walking to running, did you ever stop to think as a child, "Maybe I should stay with crawling, it's safer"?

NO!!

You hit the ground running at top speed for as long and as far as you could go.

That is the same process of flow you are in now. As you continue to uncover these inner child parts that were once exiled you will put them to use as soon as they are integrated back into you. Why would you not?!

Tools and talents are meant to be used and utilized for your greater expression and service to others.

As you continue to take these steps to uncover and learn about all those pieces and parts of you that were exiled and protected all these years, you will begin to see the greater beauty of all those around you and the amazingly bright souls of each person you interact with, because of your own awareness of your greater wisdom and knowledge from this process of self-discovery.

The more you know about yourself, the more you will appreciate and know about others. The greatest healers in the world are those who have integrated their own inner Devil, Shadow and Exiled Inner Child Parts. They have the experience of the depth of love within them, that they formerly thought of as darkness and evil. This awareness allows them to see the same love in all others with compassion and empathy. They've been there and can now guide others without judgment or criticism back into the light of love.

This journey you have taken is all about you to heal and be whole in love and light again. And once you are whole and healed, you will be ready and willing to help others in their journey of healing and integration.

The more of us on this journey helping others in their journey, the faster we can heal the world and awaken into the new world of higher love and vibration that is already here and waiting for each of us to open our eyes and hearts to it.

The Golden Age is upon us and is only an integrated and open heart away from each of us. As we heal and integrate our inner Devils, we graduate to Angels on Earth and are called to help in the awakening of the rest of our Earth Family.

You have everything you need to Understand and Utilize the inner parts of yourself that were previously hidden away. Those previously hidden parts are now your Superpowers. Use them wisely and compassionately.

Not everyone will be as ready as you are to tackle their inner Devils. Be patient and know that everyone is in perfect timing of their unique soul's journey and will gain their Superpowers in their own good time.

All you need to do is be an example of one who has done the work and is willing to show others the way when they are ready. You cannot and should not attempt to do the work for them. Your only function is that of a guide and coach. They are capable of doing their own work, but it is easier when they have a guide and coach who has already been there to let them know they are on the right track and what they are experiencing is completely normal.

Chapter Fifteen

WELCOME TO WHOLENESS

Welcome, Welcome, Welcome!!!

You made it through and are now more whole than ever before.

Enjoy your new awarenesses and feelings of being a whole and integrated human being on the new Earth of higher vibration and higher awareness.

No longer will you be living in the numb zone of life as you did before. Now life will be fuller, richer and more experiential than you've ever known it before. You will need time to adjust and get accustomed to the new you.

Those around you will also need time to adjust to the new you. However, as you are shifting and growing, you are shifting into parallel realities that better align to your new higher vibration of being. Therefore, the new dimension will be more in alignment with your new vibration, and so will all those in that new higher vibrational dimension.

As you acclimatize to your new vibration, so will the world around you, because it is a new world of higher vibrational reality already. You will feel more and more at home and comfortable in your new reality as you settle into your new wholeness.

It is very likely that you will still be aware of and able to see and occasionally interact with those at lower vibrational realities for a while, but like more new levels of experience, you will naturally move away from those of lower vibrational realities and gravitate towards those more in alignment with your new vibrational expression.

Wholeness is a magical thing, but it does take time to get used to. You will feel more emotions in a deeper way than you did previously. Do your best to not run from or stuff those emotions. Feel them and let them flow through you. Do not try to hang onto those emotions. That only blocks your energetic flow.

Your energetic flow will become more and more important to you as you raise your frequency. Allowing your natural emotions to flow through you and not trying to suppress or hang onto them, will greatly increase your natural synchronicities and sensitivities to others and the flow of universal energies.

As we journey into wholeness and higher vibrational states, energy will become our highest focus. Our ability to utilize, manipulate and generate energy will become our newest passions and purposes in the new dimensions of light, love and connection with All That Is.

Wholeness is magical and amazing, but it is still just another level on the ladder of ascension for all of us. Just as middle school and high school were amazing new experiences when it was our time to transition to them, so too will this level of wholeness become our next level of learning and growth.

The greatest detriment to wholeness is self-judgment and self-criticalness. Allowance and acceptance of all our potentials of the greatest good and greatest bad is the path through to integration and inter-relation with all others.

Do not deny any part of yourself, for every part of you that you deny is a part of another you cannot access or accept. Self-acceptance is the path to personal wholeness and integration with all others and all that is.

Your awareness and acceptance of all of you will heal you in an instant and lead you to facilitating the healing of others through your example. Be all of you as often as is appropriate and possible and you will gain more power and potential than you have ever experienced before.

As the Heart Math Institute has discovered, Authenticity is 4,000 times more powerful than Love energetically. Your authenticity lies within your wholeness and your wholeness lies directly within your acceptance and allowing of all parts of you.

Become the Superhuman that you truly are meant to be by freeing your inner exiled children, shadows and Devils from their dark corners and into the light of love, connection and integration.

The World needs you, all of you, just as you are in your unique wholeness and being. You are a special and necessary part of the whole that is the ALL. The ALL could not be the ALL That Is without you and your unique piece of creation. Be ALL that you ARE, so that the ALL can be the ALL.

You Are Loved! You Are Cherished! You Are Needed!!

EPILOGUE

I am so excited to have been on this journey with each of you and I hope I get the opportunity to meet you in the future to hear about your unique journey of "Facing the Devil in You" and the wholeness you are living now.

The Golden Age is upon us, and we each chose to be here now to experience these amazing changes and to play our part in the evolution of Humankind into the higher 4th Density or 5th Dimensional level that is now upon us.

You are integral in the evolution of the Planet into the higher dimension and higher vibrations. You are integral in the evolution of the collective consciousness from 3D awareness into 5D awareness and acceptance of our place in the Galactic Federation of Light.

We are on the precipice of acceptance into the Galactic Federation and open contact with our Intergalactic Family. This will only be possible when enough of us are living as integrated, whole and authentic humans and beings of light and love.

These are extremely exciting times to be here and the reason we all chose to come to the Hardest School in the Universe to be a part of this exciting evolution into the next higher expression of humanity from Homo Sapiens to Homo-Galactics.

Grab your toothbrushes and don't forget your towel!! We'll be starting the boarding process soon!! Next stop Orion, Alpha-Centauri, and Sirius... To Infinity and Beyond!!

I Love You All and will see you at the Launch Pad!!

REFERENCES

I f you have made it all the way here, I can only assume it is because you want to know where I learned it all.

A lot of it I always knew or felt, but I needed many teachers along the way to remind me or solidify what I always suspected. Here is a list of many of those teachers and where you can find them. It is by no means a comprehensive list, but I will do my level best to include as many as I can.

Dannion Brinkley: www.Dannion.com

A Course in Miracles: www.ACIM.org

Earl 'Raj' Purdy: www.EarlPurdy.com
(My A Course In Miracles Teacher, Brother and Friend.)

PSI Seminars: www.PSISeminars.com

Dr. Joe Dispenza: www.drjoedispenza.com

Gregg Braden: www.greggbraden.com

Daryl Anka & Bashar: www.Bashar.org

Byron Katie: www.TheWork.com

Richard Bach: www.richardbach.com
(Author of 'Illusions', 'Jonathan Livingston
Seagull', 'The Messiah's Handbook', and
many more)

Stuart Wilde: www.stuartwilde.com
(Author of 'Life Was Never Meant to Be a
Struggle', 'Silent Power', 'Infinite Self', 'Miracles',
and many more)

The Internal Family System Foundation:
www.ifs.com

Ernest Holmes: The Science of Mind:
https://scienceofmindarchives.com/
about-ernest-holmes/

Brene Brown: www.BreneBrown.com

James Redfield: https://www.celestinevision.com/
(Author of: 'The Celestine Prophecy', 'The Tenth
Insight', 'The Secrets of Shambala', and more)

I know I am forgetting so many more teachers that
I've learned from over the years, but I think I'll have to
stop here. Otherwise, I'll need a whole other book just
for References.

ACKNOWLEDGMENTS

I t is time to attempt the impossible task of thanking and acknowledging all those that have played a part in my life that led me to this moment. I know I will miss some of you and for that I do apologize in advance. Just know I haven't forgotten you and you have my deepest thanks and gratitude for whatever role you played in my life.

To Begin I will go back to the beginning and attempt this in a pseudo chronology, if I can.

Thank you to my first mentor and friend, Dannion Brinkley. Your wisdom and lessons, though unconventional, did have a huge impact on me and still do. Love you Big D!

To Earl 'Raj' Purdy, my A Course in Miracles teacher, coach, friend and partner in crime. You are a shining example of Love and what a lifetime of study and focus can do for a mere mortal. I love you, my Brother!

To my Unity Church and Science of Mind Families, thank you for all you do and for your shining example in this world.

To Karen Koebnick, who did the heavy lifting for so many years to provide the thousands of us who love you, a place to learn from the best and brightest in the world today! Thank you, thank you, thank you! We love you so much!

To Dr. Joe Dispenza, who's work in neuroscience, meditation and down-right alchemy and magic has transformed how we think about the mind, body, spirit and energy. Thank you for your dedication and near obsession with changing how we heal, create and live. You are Loved and Cherished by me and all those who have taken part in your work.

To Gregg Braden, who's teachings help us to bridge the gap of science and spirituality in a way that makes all us Whoo-Whoos feel almost normal. Thank you for your insight, music and humor over all these years.

To Daryl Anka and Bashar, thank you for the many decades of teaching us slow learning humans about our place in the universe, our true potential and what we are truly capable of. I couldn't have made this book what it is without your teachings, wisdom and insights from the higher realms. Thank you!!

To Byron Katie, Katie, Thank you for your work! Your system of Inquiry was life changing for me and so many others. The ability to question ones thoughts and investigate our own minds led me down the road to my own ah-ha's and to inevitably writing this book.

To all my PSI Seminars family in Denver, California, Hawaii and across the world; Thank you for being a huge part of my growth, learning and self-acceptance along my path. Your mission of 'World Peace One Mind at a Time' has succeeded with this one mind, for sure.

To my Be Men Brothers, you have been the Iron to sharpen my Iron and the best group of guys I've had around me in decades. I owe my sanity and sobriety in large part to your love and influence. Let's keep making our dent in the world. Better Men, Better World!

To my Main Man, My Main Rapper-Scrapper, My Partner in Crime, the one and only Kirk M. Samuels; Thank you for being my brother, friend and confidant throughout the years. We've done great things together and will continue too as long as we're both able. You're a Great Man and I'm honored to call you, my friend.

To all the countless others who have graced my life with your friendship, love and energy, Thank You from the bottom of my heart for being a part of my journey. You all made your marks and helped me to get here. I cannot name you all, but you know who you are. I love you, my friends!!